What's On
YOUR
MIND?

www.mascotbooks.com

What's On Your Mind?
A Collection of Quotes for Meditation and Reflection

For more information, please contact:
Mascot Books
620 Herndon Parkway #320
Herndon, VA 20170
info@mascotbooks.com

Library of Congress Control Number: 2020925047

CPSIA Code: PRV0321A
ISBN-13: 978-1-64307-534-1

Printed in the United States

I wish to dedicate this book to my family: my mom, Geraldine; my dad, DeCosta; and my sister, Natasha. Thank you for your encouragement in ways you may never know. I love you! To my nephew, Paul Asa Coles, Jr. and my niece, Aria Joi Coles...Your Auntie Kim loves you and prays that these words will one day be a source of inspiration on your journey into adulthood.

To my friends and church family who have liked my posts through the years. I am grateful for your support and prayers.

A special word of thanks to my sisters in Christ who prayed for me continuously to write this book: Marsha, Gail, Kimberly, Coleen, Lisa C., Lisa K., Miko, and Shyla. Your quiet inspiration and public prayers have made this work come alive! I love each of you and thank God for you.

Lastly, to a dear friend and sister Lonniece Williams. Lonniece, thank you for pushing me to take my posts and share them in this devotional. You are the reason we are reading these words today. You always nudged me and reminded me that there was a book to be born! I love you and praise God that you saw what was yet to appear. Now let your gifts make room for you...

To the reader: I pray that these words will come alive in your spirit. God has anointed His children with something to say. Never be afraid to share what's on your mind.

What's On YOUR MIND?

A Collection of Quotes for Meditation and Reflection

KIMBERLY HEADLEY

Introduction

F acebook is one of the most amazing creations on the world wide web. The moment I realized that I had another way of communicating God's word through inspired quotes, I used it to the fullest. Sometimes within a day, I would post at least five sayings to inspire my friends who may have been going through a situation.

I have friends and family members that have never thought about attending church or focusing on God. In little ways they let me know that the word I released or the saying I posted was right on time. I can only thank God for the ability to discern what someone needed to read at that very moment.

I debut this short devotional of meditations and reflections, some that are born out of my Facebook posts, with the intent of showing someone that God is ever mindful of His children. These words are just my open thoughts and reflections about the issues of life, dealings with people, and our journey with God.

For the reader, as you meditate and reflect upon these words, let it present an opportunity for you to journal what these words may be saying to you. There is space at the end of the book for you to share your own thoughts.

If you sense that God needs you to say something, remember that the Word of God has been given as your personal guide, and that the words we speak, post, and pen have been sent from the Divine

Interpreter of the human heart. I hope you enjoy this devotional and find it relevant in your daily meditation as you walk through the vicissitudes of life.

Kimberly V. Headley

Sunday

"It is not how big a step you make, it is that you just take one;
it is not how big a leap of faith you make,
it is that you leap! The faith comes in just your trying."

We seem to think that making big steps and big strides is the only way to begin a thing. For some unknown reason, we believe that operating in this way says that we are serious. Not always so. Most people are afraid to take big steps because they believe that it translates into big failure. But notice how God moved in the scriptures: He used a remnant, a small amount of people. The Big God used small groups, small things to make a statement.

It is important that we take that first step. Taking that first step means we have already made movement in the right direction.

Once you realize you are not where you were a moment ago when you took that first step, you can take another step. Now, keep stepping. Okay, so maybe you are not a stepper but a leaper. Leaping means that you jump. The same concept applies: before you leap big, leap small—one leap at a time. The power and the success behind your step or leap qualifies as Faith. It takes faith to even believe that a step can be made and that a leap can be evident. Just trying makes the difference between those who say that they will and those who actually do. So, remember it is not the size of the step or the leap, but the faith in attempting it in the first place. You never know what will follow if you don't at least try!

"One day the apostles said to the Lord, 'We need more faith; tell us how to get it.'"
—Luke 17:5 (TLB)

Monday

"Let your love of God be contagious enough for someone to catch!"
Hachew! #Godblessyou

When we catch a cold, it easily spreads germs. We touch so many things in our daily living that it is easy to become susceptible to colds and cold-like symptoms. There is really no cure for the common cold, but there are certain home remedies that can be used to rid oneself of it. But when it comes to the love of Christ, God wants you to be "contaminated," so to speak, by Jesus's love and what His love can do to you. God wants us to be so enamored with His Son for the purpose of catching the influence of His love so that it will invade our bodies and make us over into His image and likeness.

Love, according to the scriptures, covers a multitude of sins. Picture the contagion of love incubating your soul so much that you begin to love the unlovable; that you would sacrifice your life to love in any way imaginable. The gospel group, Commissioned, sings a song that says, "love isn't love, 'til you've given it away." What has your love infected today? God's love came down and rescued us and healed us from the disease of sin.

So, let the love of God that now lives in you be susceptible to the sinful lives that draw us away from God. Someone needs to catch the love bug so that they can be touched by the healing hands of the Father.

"Real love isn't our love for God, but his love for us. God sent his Son to be the sacrifice by which our sins are forgiven."

—1 John 4:10 (CEV)

Tuesday

"Jesus is requesting to be more than your friend!"

F acebook is famous for its "friend request" model. The one way that you gain access to people is by "friending" them. Most people probably choose to accept friend requests from people who are friends of their friends. When we accept a friend request, we invite our new friend to have access to our page, which tells a bit about who we are. Even though we may accumulate hundreds of Facebook friends, the reality is that those who know us well usually comprise of a small sector of people.

Jesus already knows who we are! He is not asking us to invite Him to be a friend; that would categorize Him with all of the other "friends" you have. Jesus is a "friend that sticks closer than a brother," who is more than a click away. You can call on Him day or night and He will answer. But He desires to be more than your friend; He wants to be Your Lord. Lordship means that He is in full control of your life. Friendship means that you share a common bond with your friends, but any commonality with Christ must produce individuality in you.

Jesus doesn't do ordinary things. He operates in the extraordinary. Give Him the opportunity to be more than just someone who visits your page every now and then. He wants to write a new page in your book that doesn't begin with the word "Face." Honor His request, and when you make your requests known to Him, He will honor yours according to His will and purpose for your life.

"Greater love hath no man than this that a man lay down his life for his friends."

—John 15:13 (KJV)

Wednesday

"Tough times call for the school of kneeology."

#pray

J esus is the epitome of our divine prayer warrior who teaches us how to pray, or communicate, to Him. Jesus was teaching each of us through the scripture in Luke 18:1 that we are to always pray and not give up until the answer comes; this means that we should continue to flood heaven with our prayers. As believers who are called to a life of prayer, we are to pray, petition, and ask, believing that our prayers will be answered in God's time. What the outcome looks like is not our business, but God's.

It is easy for us to pray casual prayers when things are going well. But let a difficult situation arise and we find ourselves driven to our knees in desperation. God does not want us to come to Him in prayer only when there is trouble. Instead, always seek Him and His direction through prayer.

We have plenty of biblical examples of those men and women who prayed or petitioned God in some way. We may not have always read that they fell on their knees, but our Lord shows us how to fall on our knees as He did in the Garden of Gethsemane (Mark 14:32). The Garden of Gethsemane was the place of preparation for Jesus's offering His life to a flawed humanity. It was in the Garden of Gethsemane where He decided that the will of the Father would be the will for His life in order to save the world. This divine encounter with heaven prepared Jesus for the most important moment of His life: the crucifixion.

Whenever Jesus arose or left the place of prayer, He entered a posture of power. Miracles followed His times of prayer. What will follow yours? Don't stop praying!

"One day Jesus told his disciples a story to illustrate their need for constant prayer and to show them that they must keep praying until the answer comes."
—Luke 18:1 (TLB)

Thursday

"God didn't give Abraham a plan; He gave him a promise."

W e make promises to people that we end up breaking because we made them. Anything fashioned by the hands of mankind has the power to be broken. God, on the other hand, gave Abraham a promise and the promise He gave can never be broken because what God gives, God has the power to make good on it. He told Abraham to try to count the sand on the seashore and the stars in the sky. Abraham couldn't provide Him with numbers because there were too many of them. What is God saying? We will never outdo what God wants to do in our lives. So, we have to recognize that His promises will always outweigh our plans because His promises to us are not contingent on our plans that we make toward Him.

God's promises will always prevail because He strategized them that way. In the case of Abraham, God prophesied that Abraham would have a son, in his old age and past the age of Sarah's childbearing years. Sarah also wrestled with the fact that she was barren. How would this prophecy come to pass? Since Abraham had no idea when the promise would be fulfilled, Abraham overstepped God by creating a plan with Sarah to impregnate an innocent slave girl. As a result, problems crept in.

We waste so much time perfecting our plans while forsaking

God's promises. To fulfill His promises requires us to embrace two basic words: faith and trust. A word to the wise: Keep your plans out of God's promise!

"For when God made a promise to Abraham, because he could swear by no greater, he sware by himself... And so, after he had patiently endured, he obtained the promise."
—Hebrews 6:13,15 (KJV)

Friday

"Jesus is looking for the Bride of His Church, not the first lady."

We never see it referenced in the Scriptures that Jesus calls the church His first lady. When we think of a first lady, we typically look at the President of the United States's wife. Then the second reference to a first lady is the wife of the pastor of the church. While the title "first lady" has its respective place in government and in the church, it will never take the place of the Bride. Jesus died to make the church His Bride. The Bride of Christ is to be spotless, which is not a requirement for the first lady. The first lady is supposed to be by a pastor's side. She is to look the part of being the trophy piece of the pastor. Sometimes the title "first lady" can be offensive because it reduces the worth and the intelligence of the woman whose title it surrounds.

We do not always see what our first ladies are worth because most often they are in the shadow of their husbands. But not the Bride of Christ. She is the center of attention as she processes the aisle of salvation on her way to Her Husband, The Lord Jesus Christ. When the Bride comes into the room, all eyes are on her, not because of what she is wearing but who she is! She is offered to her groom.

So, the next time you want to equate yourself with being a first lady, remember the first lady doesn't necessarily mean that you are the only lady, but the Bride of Christ is the only one He loves and died for!

"Then I saw New Jerusalem, that holy city, coming down from God in heaven. It was like a bride dressed in her wedding gown and ready to meet her husband."

—Revelation 21:2 (CEV)

Saturday

"You have looked in the mirror long enough, now believe who you see!"

#imagodei

We are made in the image of God. When God said in Genesis 1, "Let us make humankind in our image and according to our likeness," He intended for us to possess the essence of His character. Even though there are God attributes that we will never possess, like Sovereignty, Omniscience, and Omnipotence, there are some characteristics about us that have been made in the image of God, and those we are to manifest. The mirror of life we stare into daily shows us two things: who we are and who we are not. While the mirror reflects a live picture of who we are, mirrors can deceive and have you believing some things about you that are not true.

Have you stood in front of the mirror that made you heavier than you appeared to be, or much taller when you are actually much shorter? Well, in God's mirror, He wants His creation to be content with the way they have been created. You and I are original designs from Heaven. Although God knew exactly what we would look like physically, He was even more certain of our image spiritually. We are supposed to reflect the imago dei and embrace what God has already affirmed when He made us in His image. It takes believing what we see when we really look at ourselves, not the person that others speak negatively about. Believing what you see means you also accept what you believe you have seen.

So, without apology, believe in the image that stares back at you for it is God revealing Himself through you and in you. Seeing is believing when you see through the imago dei.

"And as we have born the image of the earthly, so shall we bear the image of the heavenly."
—1 Corinthians 15:49 (GNV)

Sunday

"Truth is a constant that can never be changed by a lie."

J esus told the disciples in John 8:32 "and ye shall know the truth and the truth shall make you free." So, if the truth makes us free, what will a lie do? Keep us in bondage. God is the Truth that is never changing and unending. There is one absolute in life, and that is God. He defeated the lie that was told in the Garden when mankind was tricked by the serpent. Although they suffered punishment, it was clear and evident that once God revealed the Truth of His Word, redemption was put in motion to deliver us from the lie we believed for a brief moment in time.

So, salvation becomes crucial for us to be connected to Truth. Just like darkness cannot overtake light, a lie can never change the truth. Truth comes to reveal the lie and its ineffectiveness against a person who has taken that principle in John 8 and made it applicable to their lives.

"Of his own will begat he us with the word of truth, that we should be a kind of firstfruits of his creatures."
—James 1:18 (KJV)

Monday

"God does not suffer from memory loss. He chooses to forget.
So, if He chooses to forget about the things you and I have done,
why can't we choose to forget what others have done to us?
I choose to forgive and I choose to forget."

P erhaps one of the most difficult acts of "kindness" we can express
is the ability to forgive! It is much easier to rehearse the pain
than to erase it so we can enter into peace. We have heard it said
that forgiveness is not for the other person, but for us. If we examine
this statement clearly, it makes a lot of sense. Oftentimes, the person
whom we believe owes us an apology for the pain they have caused is
probably not thinking about what they have done, let alone admitting
to what they have done. So, I would agree with the originator of this
statement that forgiveness is for us because we are the ones living
with the affliction.

Jesus made a very definitive statement about the act of forgiving
in Luke. Peter asked how many times we are to forgive someone
who wrongs us. The Lord's reply was "seventy times seven," which
means that we are not to count how many times we forgive someone.
Instead, just forgive them. This is the moral of the inference made by
Jesus. If we literally count how many times we forgive someone, then
are we really forgiving or are we trying to keep them accountable

to the pain, or are we trying to make them measure up to our standard of forgiveness? When we say "enough" apologizing or "enough" accepting their forgiveness, then we have forgiven. No! "Seventy times seven" equals 490 times. Think about it: who is going to recall 490 instances when they have forgiven a person? No one. This is why our Lord commands us not only to love, but to forgive.

Our Father in Heaven did not count the numerous instances when we have done unforgivable things. He loves and forgives. If the Lord were to pull out a chart of sins we committed, we would think twice about who we will forgive, causing us to exercise wisdom by choosing to forgive them and their transgressions and move on... forget about it. I choose to forgive and forget! Do the same.

"And forgive us our debts, as we forgive our debtors."
—Matthew 6:12 (KJV)

Tuesday

"You are as faithful as your last promise kept."

P romises are made and, unfortunately, broken by us all the time. It would be wonderful to think that if I make a promise, I intend on keeping it. But a couple of things happen: either I made a promise that I never intended to keep, or I earnestly wanted to keep the promise but just could not. Sadly, we are in the category of the former for several reasons. Some of us just like hearing ourselves talk. Some of us just like giving people "a line." Some of us just think that we have the power within our control to make these promises in the first place.

The exciting news today for you about promises is...drumroll: God keeps His promises to each of us. No matter the number of promises that have been made by Jehovah, He responds to them and, as a result, we have never felt the absence of a broken promise. Promises, I believe, are connected to faithfulness because our keeping a promise would suggest that we intend to see it come to pass. We are faithful to guard it, making sure that it does become a fulfillment of a desire we have.

So, the next time you make a promise, remember how God responds to promises: Yea and Amen! If you cannot do the same, it would be best not to make a promise at all.

"May the Lord, your ancestors' God, continue to multiply you—a thousand times more! And may God bless you, just as he promised."

—Deuteronomy 1:11 (CEB)

Wednesday

"What God has called us to, He will prepare us for!"

God has been calling on humanity since the beginning of time. When God called out to Adam in the cool of the day, it was because Adam was not in the place, the presence of God, that he was supposed to be. Sin brought the disconnection. As a result, we have not realized the calling that God has for us, first to salvation, and then to purpose and destiny until He introduces Jesus in Genesis 3:15 as the seed of the woman who crushes the serpent's head: "And I will put enmity between you and the woman, and between your offspring and hers; he will crush your head, and you will strike his heel."

God does not rely on each of us to put the characteristics of the call together, nor does He hope that we can fulfill the call. When He calls us, He plans to equip us in every way to succeed since He knows that we do not have what it takes to manifest the call. Think about it. When has God ever expected you to do the part that only He can do? If we are honest with ourselves, we'll admit that there are times when we attempt to do God's job. When we realize that we are over our heads, we must return to the source of all power and all knowledge—the Father above who knows all things and has the ability to see everything He desires for your life come to fruition.

If you find yourself feeling a tremendous burden on your shoulders because you're overwhelmed by the enormity of the call, remember that God does the preparing. Don't be surprised by what He will use and whom He will use to get you to the appointed place He has called you to.

"Adam, where are you?" Your reply ought to be, "Here am I Lord, send me."

"And he called unto him the twelve, and began to send them forth by two and two; and gave them power over unclean spirits."
—Mark 6:7 (KJV)

Thursday

"When people point the finger at your sin, point your finger to the Cross.
He paid for it already! Hallelujah.
It doesn't mean that you abuse what He did!
You are grateful for what Jesus did.
Pointing fingers of condemnation will never be greater than
nail pierced hands of salvation."

Y ou may recall those who pointed you out as the guilty culprit during moments in your childhood. You may also recall how the "pointed finger" evoked the worst feeling ever.

Fortunately, God has provided an answer to the pointed fingers of condemnation and judgment that come from people who want you to be guilty of a crime, who want you to experience shame and embarrassment for being found out. Thank God for Jesus Christ who came into the world to save it, not to condemn it, according to John 3:17 ("For God did not send his Son into the world to condemn the world, but to save the world through him."). It is easy for each of us to point out what is wrong. Why not try looking at what is right or can be right in a person's life?

So, for those who continue to feel the pointed finger of condemnation, remind yourself that the Cross of Christ covered all of your sins; and the nail-pierced hands that drew precious blood have more than enough power to erase the stain of sin. The woman caught in adultery had fingers pointing out her sins. But when she met Jesus, He stooped down, and with His finger rewrote her story.

God wants to do the same for you. There is no condemnation to those who are in Christ Jesus according to Romans 8:1. God is not pointing His finger; He is extending His hand.

"So now there is no condemnation for those who belong to Christ Jesus."

—Romans 8:1 (NLT)

Friday

A friend request that can't be denied:
"Greater love hath no man than this,
that a man lay down his life for his friends."

—John 15:13

I t is interesting how on Facebook you can receive friend requests from people that you do not know. Oftentimes, the person requesting to be your friend has a mutual Facebook friend in common with you.

But what if you accept a friend request with no connection to any of your friends and it is a random friend request? Do you still accept or do you reject it because you do not know them? Most often when I do get those kinds of requests, I automatically reject them because I do not know the ulterior motive of this individual wanting to be my friend.

What if Jesus sent you a friend request? Would you act as though you know Him or would you pretend as if you are not aware of who He is and just ignore His friend request? Beloved, the latter would be a foolish thing to do, especially for a believer.

Jesus tells His disciples in John 15 that He is the true vine. The connection to the Father comes through the Son. So, just like a friend request connects individuals to each other, we can connect to God through Jesus. Friend requests are a choice. On a spiritual level, there are people who want to get close to God but do not want to accept Jesus's friend request to get there.

Rejecting Jesus is the worst mistake anyone could ever make. He gave His life to show His love is the greatest. It was not a request of yours. Instead, you are the recipient of His extraordinary sacrifice.

"You didn't choose me. I chose you. I appointed you to go and produce lasting fruit, so that the Father will give you whatever you ask for, using my name."

—John 15:16 (NLT)

Saturday

"Don't hate the dreamer who sees the dream
as so much more than what could be."

From the very beginning, God gave us the ability to dream. Look at Joseph in the book of Genesis. Through dreams, he was shown how God would use his life in order to save the children of Israel. Joseph could not see this right away, and his brothers avoided the dreams as much as possible because they presumed that Joseph was boasting when in fact, he was just believing without really seeing. We call that faith.

What about your dreams? When God gives you a dream, do not worry about those who cannot see the potential outcome of the dream because they are not a part of the dream. In some cases, there may be those who are designated to be recipients of dreams, whether as believers joyfully celebrating the fruition of your dream, or as doubters whose eyes may finally open to believing that with God all things are indeed possible.

Whatever God has given to you in a vision or a dream, do not think that God needs your extra help to make the dream become a reality. Trust God to bring to pass the seed, the vision, the dream that He has planted in your heart.

Joseph had no idea what was coming his way. Instead, he elected to look to his Father to be the sustainer and keeper of the dream. At the appropriate time, it was released and it changed an entire generation of people.

Do not be afraid to dream!

"'Are you indeed to reign over us? Are you indeed to have dominion over us?' So they hated him even more because of his dreams and his words."

—Genesis 37:8 (NRSV)

Sunday

"You cannot deal with unreasonable people with reason.
You must pray."

Have you ever met a person who was so unreasonable that you could not get through to them? No matter how much you tried to help them understand a situation, they only heard and listened to their viewpoint? Reason would be a wonderful additive to unreasonable persons, only if they were willing to listen. The unreasonableness forces you to make a decision. Will you allow the unreasonable nature of the person to drive you to a place of frustration, or will you incorporate wisdom and pray?

That's it…pray. God gave us the gift of prayer, communicating with Him when those we attempt to communicate with are not hearing what we are trying to convey. When you come to the point of praying about the person and the matter at hand, you will find a sense of peace that will lead you to accept the unreasonableness of the person in question. In other words, leave them and the situation in the hands of God. You have prayed about it; this is the most reasonable thing you can do.

"Listen to the sound of my cry, my King and my God, for to you I pray."
—Psalm 5:2 (NRSV)

Monday

"If you are going to pledge an allegiance, it should be to the Lord."

When I was in grade school, every morning at class assembly we had to stand up and recite the Pledge of Allegiance. With hands on our hearts and mouths resounding with patriotic pride, we really did not understand the depth of the Pledge of Allegiance and what it meant; we just stated it because we were supposed to. In America in 2016, we saw this allegiance being pledged to our beloved America, who is guilty of so many crimes of hate; an America who did not allow me to feel the patriotism because I was experiencing racism because of the color of my skin. But when a relationship with Christ was offered to me by the Savior himself, I had to recognize that my allegiance would not be to a flag, a political party, an ideology, but my allegiance was to the Savior of my soul. When I place my hand over my heart, I am letting Him know that this is the place where I house Him.

It is so easy to get wrapped up in traditions and mindsets that cause you to stand in allegiance and agreement because it seems to be the politically correct thing to do. But take an assessment of what happened when your allegiances proved to be a false sense of security and hope, when you recognized that the moral tenets of our country do not have the power to transform your life. If anything, it conforms you to the power that rules the system that has been designed to keep you at bay. This is why we need to only focus on the kingdom of the Lord and nothing else. Sadly, when we repeat "one nation under God, indivisible, with liberty and justice for all," it does not mean liberty and justice for all…it means that I make my God be a god of my color, my condition, my complacency, and my unwillingness to change.

"On that day there will be five cities in the land of Egypt that speak the language of Canaan and swear allegiance to the Lord of hosts. One of these will be called the City of the Sun."
—Isaiah 19:18 (NRSV)

Tuesday

"Some people lie so much they haven't realized
that Truth has told on them."

We used to chant this line in school: "Liar, liar pants on fire…"
Some people lie so much you would think that they would
buy fireproof pants to keep them from being consumed. How does
God feel about lying? Well, He named it as one of the abominations
listed in Proverbs 6:16–18: "There are six things the Lord hates—no,
seven things He detests: haughty eyes, a lying tongue, hands that kill
the innocent, a heart that plots evil, feet that race to do wrong…"
Simply put, God hates lying so much because it is contrary to the
truth. According to John 8:32, the truth makes us free: "Then you will
know the truth, and the truth will set you free."

Lying keeps us in bondage. There is one thing truth and a lie
cannot do and that is exist in the same space. Truth comes to expose
and reveal, and when the truth manifests, one who lies cannot help
but begin to tell the truth. Remember Adam and Eve in the garden?
When God asked where Adam was, he replied that he hid himself
because he was naked. What happened in that moment was this:
Adam could not lie to the Lord. It was evident that truth caused him
to reveal the condition he was in. He told God, "I am naked." But then
a lie tried to keep him in darkness because he did not want to tell the

whole truth, which was that he disobeyed God. Instead, he gave an excuse and blamed God for the transgression when God asked him if he ate from the forbidden tree: "the woman you gave me, gave it to me and I did eat…"

Beloved, we must learn to recognize that God's truth is a revealer of secrets. We will never outsmart God when it comes to exposing lies. The reason why the truth makes you free when you are honest is that lying puts and keeps you in bondage. And once you tell one lie then you have to cover the lie with another lie, and it keeps snowballing.

Ultimately, lying before God represents the exact opposite of the truth. Lying makes one willing to accept second best; it also causes people who do it often to believe that this form of behavior is acceptable to God. Lying perpetuates falsehood, and God wants nothing to do with anything that is contrary to His truth.

"The Lord is near to all who call on him, to all who call on him in truth."

—Psalm 145:18 (NRSV)

Wednesday

"Being grateful doesn't require your words, it requires your actions."

"How can I say thanks for the things you have done for me, things so undeserved, yet you gave to prove your love for me..." These words are from one of Andrae Crouch's famous songs, "My Tribute." It is a song of celebration and thanksgiving to God for what Christ has done. The songwriter demonstrates gratitude to God for all that God has done. Mr. Crouch is not thankful for what God has said, but what has been done on his and our behalf.

So, when I think about gratefulness being extended from me toward God, my response must be an act rather than a mere "thank you." My "thank you" does not have to be spoken, but perhaps it could reveal itself through my actions: how I live my life as a Christian, how I demonstrate kindness and love to others, and how I do my best to honor God the best way I can. These are just a few ways that I can let God know how grateful I am for all God has done for me. Every day I rise and when I fall to my knees to say, "thank you," I am just responding in gratitude to Christ for blessing me to see another day as the old folks would say, "in the land of the living."

"Be anxious for nothing, but in everything, by prayer and supplication with gratitude, make your requests known to God."
—Psalm 4:6 (MEV)

Thursday

"You never really know what you are capable of doing
until you find yourself doing it."

I once heard a televangelist say that if we have a fear of doing something, then "do it afraid." Many of us have found ourselves in predicaments when we have to perform an uncomfortable task. Although the task is irrelevant, what IS relevant is our mindset that believes we are going to fail, we are going to embarrass ourselves, we are going to bring shame to our families, the companies, or teams we represent.

Well, say no more. God has the awesome ability to get us to do something without us even knowing that we are doing it. It is just like when you first learned to ride a bike. When I was learning how to ride my bike there was someone alongside me to make sure I didn't tumble. Before I realized that my helper quietly left my side, I found myself confidently pedaling my bike without training wheels.

In the Gospels, Peter had a similar encounter with Jesus. The disciples were all on the boat and Peter saw an image, which looked like Jesus out on the water. He said to the Lord, "Lord if that is you, bid me come." Jesus replied, "Come." It was not long after that Peter stepped out of the boat and walked on the water toward Jesus. Peter had no idea that he would be walking on water. He just found himself doing it because his faith gave him the push to respond to the Lord's authority.

Whatever the assignment or task, do not focus on your inadequacies before you even give it a try. Don't talk yourself out of what would be an opportunity to praise God because He is the only reason why you are capable of doing what you consider to be impossible.

"For nothing will be impossible with God."
—Luke 1:37 (NASB)

Friday

"When life gives you lemons, make sweet tea!"

How many people love lemonade over sweet tea? Lemonade, of course, tastes good only when it is sweetened. What about your life? What has you sour that you need something to sweeten it? Many of us find ourselves in troublesome situations that just leave us sour, bitter, and tart.

You ever see the strangest faces a person makes when they suck on a piece of lemon? For some of you, life has done the same thing. You have sucked on an unhealthy relationship; you have sucked on the disappointment of your children; you have sucked on the firing from your job of fifteen years; you have sucked on wanting to live a different kind of life, but feeling stuck in the one you are in. No need to fear, the sweet tea is here.

Sweet tea just leaves a refreshing taste in your mouth. Southern sweet tea is perhaps the best tea, because the way it is brewed and served just makes you forget everything that makes you feel not so sweet. Jesus is like that; His is the sweetest name that can turn a sour situation into a sweet sensation. Jesus is so powerful in His ability to make you feel joy again. He is like the sweet tea that has a piece of lemon in it. It doesn't matter how tart the lemon tastes on its own, because immersed in the sweet tea, it never overpowers the tea, but submits to the potency of the sweetness. Same thing with Jesus. It doesn't matter what life throws your way, Jesus can change the bitter to the sweet, if He chooses to.

"How sweet are Your words to my taste! Yes, sweeter than honey to my mouth!"
—Psalm 119:103 (NASB)

Saturday

"Ministry is not to be convenient or comfortable.
As a matter of fact, we are called to be inconvenienced and
uncomfortable."

There is absolutely nothing convenient or comfortable about Jesus's life story and ministry. As a matter of fact, Jesus was born into a family He did not ask for and in a place that He had no control over. He was born at a time when a wicked King sought to destroy His life because of who He was and what He thought Jesus was destined to become. There was nothing convenient or comfortable about the early years of His life.

What about you? Have you been inconvenienced or made uncomfortable in any part of your life? How did you respond? How do you feel now? Do you recognize that it may be time for something new to happen? When you get to this stage, you really start agreeing with God that you can afford to be inconvenienced and made uncomfortable because you love Him. Being inconvenienced and made uncomfortable is necessary for what God has designed for your life in ministry. And if you are honest, you have allowed yourself to be inconvenienced and made uncomfortable with persons who never deserved that time or attention.

Whatever Jesus asks of you, just as He asked Peter three times of his love for Jesus, Peter was about to be inconvenienced and made uncomfortable. Peter would have to take a journey that he may not have wanted to…somewhere down the line, after the great miracles and proclamations he would render in the book of Acts. But in the end, he died an honorable death unto the Lord and whatever inconvenience or discomfort he experienced would all be worth it after all!

"Then, calling the crowd to join his disciples, he said, 'If any of you wants to be my follower, you must give up your own way, take up your cross, and follow me.'"
—Mark 8:34 (NLT)

Sunday

"Everybody wants to be a judge
until they are called to the stand themselves."

The Bible tells us to judge not. No judging. No pointing of fingers. No accusations. Judgment belongs to God. Why do you believe this is so? Because we cannot be impartial in our judging. We are incapable of judging rightly 24/7 because of our partiality. We are just as guilty in our criticism of others as they are in their criticism of us.

What I appreciate about the courtroom of God, our Chief Judge, is that He is merciful. He renders a verdict not based on evidence, but because of His mercy. When we are called to His witness stand, we open ourselves up to be honest in God's presence. In the earthly courtroom, at one time, people were used to putting one hand on a Bible while holding the other hand up, promising to tell the truth, the whole truth, and nothing but the truth. Sadly, all have not lived up to the promise of telling the truth.

When you are called to the stand, remember God's mercy, which is always shown to you. We do not deserve it, yet He offers it willingly. So, the next time you want to judge someone for their actions, remember how God chose not to judge you for yours. He chooses to forgive instead. Exercise the same right to others.

"Do not judge others, and you will not be judged."
—Matthew 7:1 (NLT)

Monday

*"You may not see the fruit right away but even a seed has to be
planted.
We want the seedless fruit,
what has been manufactured and what is not authentic.
Wait on the Lord and stop being anxious."*

God is not vested in any imitation. He is real, and He wants us to be real as well. Anything counterfeit is a sign that you desire what is real, but you are not choosing to wait on its manifestation. So, you accept a cheap imitation. Oh, yes, the devil is good at imitating, and some of the things he may do may cause you to believe that it is God; however, there is always that small element of difference that may not be visible to the human eye that lets you know it is not real.

Some of you have planted many seeds in this season of your life and you are wondering when will the fruit sprout up. And because you are anxious and are exhibiting signs of presumption through your actions, you are saying to God that the real thing is taking too long and that you are just going to settle for the imitation.

If we look at a piece of fruit, for instance a tangerine, we know that tangerines have seeds. But there are these little delicious tangerines called Cuties and they have no seeds. They are the sweetest tangerines I have ever tasted. In fact, it wouldn't be unusual for me to devour about five of them in one sitting. So, my question is this: Why aren't there seeds in this tangerine, and how was it made since there are no seeds? Seeds are for the earth and the ground; they are to be watered so that the fruits and vegetables can sprout up. But if there is nothing to rise up from it, I would conclude that my fruit may possibly be a delicious imitation of the real thing and perhaps genetically manufactured. So, what am I saying to God then? That what I have may be the best, and this will do, this will suffice.

God's promise for you is worth the investment of your time and attention. God does not need any imitations, so don't settle for any.

"Imitate me, just as I also imitate Christ."
—1 Corinthians 11:11 (NKJV)

Tuesday

"No pretense in God's presence…keep it real!"

S ometimes people put up facades to mask the pain they are secretly experiencing for fear of being called weak. God is not concerned about your weakness. He already knows. He wants you to dismantle the facade because that is what is standing in the way of you seeing yourself and encountering the God that Heals. Masks may hide your face, but somewhere in your life the pain will be exposed.

God wants to deliver us from living pretentious lives. We spend so much time trying to convince everyone else that we are okay when we are falling apart on the inside. Let yourself appreciate the beauty of being weak in God's presence, being vulnerable, relying upon God's strength. Others will create an expectation of how you are to handle the pain, but God does not put an expectation on you when it comes to pain. He asks that you let Him heal you. If there were to be any expectations, it would be God placing it upon Himself because He knows He is the only Power that can Heal.

Let no one make you feel small because of the pain you feel. We may handle it differently, but only the Lord is the Healer.

"I have seen his ways, and will heal him."
—Isaiah 57:18a (NKJV)

Wednesday

"If you are actually sad that a bad relationship has come to an end,
then I question whether you know a good one when you see it.
The Lord did you a favor!
Thank Him for the further misery He spared you."

There is a song that was very popular in the 1970s that had a familiar phrase: "Breaking up is hard to do." When you love someone, and you do not see yourself apart from them, breaking up is hard to do. Why? Because in your mind, the love should be strong enough to hold the two of you together. So, what happens in a situation when you know the relationship is bad and it probably should come to an end, but you have regrets? What are you saying to the Lord in this moment that questions your response to the breakup?

God desires His best for you. Yes, the Lord is against divorce, but He has permitted divorce amongst humanity. The problem is that many of us stay in bad relationships because we do not want to violate the Lord's covenant with us when it comes to marriage. If you are honest with yourself, you will begin to recognize that the covenant had already been violated when the love for that person dissolved or disappeared. God's covenants with His people are covenants that are based on love, mutual respect, honor, and commitment. If these factors are missing in your relationship with a significant other, then you run the risk of seeing the same response replicated in your walk with the Lord.

So, in those instances when God steps in to sever the ties to what you have been dealing with, and you regret putting to an end the very thing that caused you heartache and bitterness from the beginning but feel tempted to believe that the breakup was designed to steal your joy and take away your peace, ask God to help you stand by the decision that has been made, and use no opportunity to return to it. You were spared the misery for a reason. Take the escape route and tell the Lord, "Thank You!"

"No matter what happens, always be thankful, for this is God's will for you who belong to Christ Jesus."
—1 Thessalonians 5:18 (TLB)

Thursday

"Never prostitute your integrity for power with man.
You will unleash whoredom in your ministry,
meaning you will always be for sale!"
#doitGod'sway

T here is nothing wonderful about being for sale. Yes, we have been bought with a price by our Lord Jesus Christ. But His purchase of us was never meant to pimp us into salvation. Woe unto those who think that compromising your integrity will gain you access to kingdom authority.

You may have influence over men, and when you do, you give men the power to hijack any ounce of power you may have. You will be at the mercy of men instead of operating in the favor of God until you choose to do it His way. Whoredom will always label you as available for all the wrong reasons because you have allowed yourself to be reduced as worthless.

Regain your self-respect and give your integrity the gift of authenticity. Just because you may have been for sale before does not mean that you have to continue to be sold. If you are going to be sold, be sold out for Jesus.

"God paid a great price for you. So use your body to honor God."
—1 Corinthians 6:20 (CEV)

Friday

"You have to live with yourself...so you might as well learn to love yourself."

" Learning to love yourself, it is the greatest love of all." This portion of lyrics is taken from George Benson's "Greatest Love of All," which was made famous in the late 1990s by Whitney Houston. When you love yourself, you can live with yourself because you view yourself the way God views you. We were created in His image and likeness, and we were created in love. You and I cannot come out of our skin, even though there may be times when that is the appropriate response, especially when we have messed up. No one honestly seeks disappointing God, so when it occurs, we sometimes condemn ourselves to the point that when the Lord offers you forgiveness, it becomes hard to accept because you just cannot seem to live with what you have done.

God says to you: "I love you in spite of what you think you have to live with. I love you beyond what you are willing to accept about your failures. They do not have to be a part of the glorious future that I have in store for you. You cannot escape you and who you are to me. The enemy wants you to believe who you are not. If you do, you would not be able to resolve that you can love yourself even when you feel you have to live with yourself. I know exactly who you are.

Now let me show you how to live with yourself and love yourself into the change you want to see."

"The second most important commandment says: 'Love others as much as you love yourself.' No other commandment is more important than these."

—Mark 12:31 (CEV)

Saturday

"It's not about you, so stop making it about you; it's all about Him, and when we remember that, He will keep us from falling."

P ride is a dangerous demon that can grip anyone's heart; we all must ask God to teach us humility so that we never think more highly of ourselves than we ought. Satan learned this lesson to the demise of his position in heaven but to the advantage of his earthly influence over humanity. Because pride has no set target on its radar, it looks for opportunities to trip any individual up; we would do well to recognize that we are nothing apart from God.

You may have heard some people say that we do not have to think so lowly of ourselves that we are practically invisible. Well, I would rather be categorized in such a manner than to be foolish enough to set myself next to Jesus. In Matthew 20:21, two of his disciples had a mother who requested of Jesus to allow her sons to sit on either side of Him in heaven. She had no idea what she was asking of the Lord. The Lord had to let her know that though her desire may have been well intentioned, her sons were not ready for nor capable of giving up their lives for all of humanity. There is only One Savior, and His hand stretches wide enough and deep enough to preserve lives. Therefore, it will always be and only be about Jesus who is able to keep us from stumbling.

"Do nothing from selfish ambition or conceit, but in humility count others more significant than ourselves."
—Philippians 2:3 (ESV)

Sunday

"We ought not spend time rehearsing our sins or replaying anyone else's,
especially since God has redeemed us from them."

I love these words: redeemed, restored, and refreshed. These words are God's do over for each of us who transgress. We have the tendency to remind ourselves and others of ours and their shortcomings.

Do overs are great if they are led by God. If we control our do overs, we cause us more harm than good. Why? Because then we are making ourselves solely responsible for the outcome of our do overs when we were the reason why they did not work out in the first place—we must have been doing something wrong.

If you did not measure up or meet the mark, do not replay what you have done before yourself or God. Sometimes we become our own worst enemies because we rehearse our failures over and over again. When we submit to God and allow God's power to overshadow our mistakes, He will keep us from becoming a laughingstock. This is where redemption becomes the lifeline to our do overs. Redemption makes God responsible for the process of our do overs and it makes us liable to submit to the power of redemption. Thank God for the redemptive power of a do over.

"...and are justified by his grace as a gift, through the redemption that is in Christ Jesus."
—Romans 3:24 (ESV)

Monday

"The enormity of God's love should challenge us to love unselfishly."

G igantic, huge, grandiose...these are words that describe God's love toward us. It is enormous; it is without boundary of time or space. God's love is timeless; it has no beginning or end. God's love is not of this world. This world's love has limitations and restrictions, but God's love knows no boundaries.

So, if we are called to love as God loves, then why do we box love in? Why do we hinder love's ability to be expansive, magnanimous, and unconditional? John the Apostle said in 1 John 4:20, "Whoever says, 'I love God' but hates his brother is a liar. The one who does not love his brother whom he has seen cannot love the God whom he has not seen." This is loving selfishly. When we love with prejudice, when we love exclusively, we are saying that we have the right to control whom love touches when, instead, we are called to love unselfishly.

Unselfish demonstration of love means that there is nothing we wouldn't do to experience love at its apex. Selfish love produces self-centered motivations. Open wide your heart and let agape love in.

"Dear friends, let us continuously love one another, because love comes from God. Everyone who loves has been born from God and knows God."

—1 John 4:7 (ISV)

Tuesday

*"Resist the temptation to desire again
something that God has taken from you."*

Temptations are not to be entertained but resisted. We learned early on from Adam and Eve this valuable lesson, and creation has been paying the price ever since. Desire is a powerful force that beckons temptation if the desire is viewed in a negative light.

Each of us has a vice. We have a weakness, something that easily draws us away. When God reveals what that is to you, ask the Holy Spirit to be the guardian of your heart, mind, and spirit, so that you do not return to the thing that God says for you to flee from. The enemy is waiting with subtle enticements to trap you and cause you to fall before the presence of God. Whatever he is presenting is not worth losing over all that you have gained in God. The Lord took it from you for a reason because He knows it will destroy you. It will cripple your destiny and will ruin your integrity before God and those who look to you for guidance and strength. You are human, yes, but you are also divine. Somewhere in your make-up, there is a resilient power that enables you to resist what you want so desperately.

Trust God in those weak moments. The temptation is not worth the trouble and desire is not worth the destruction.

"There isn't any temptation that you have experienced which is unusual for humans. God, who faithfully keeps His promises, will not allow you to be tempted beyond your power to resist. But when you are tempted, He will also give you the ability to endure the temptation as your way of escape."
—1 Corinthians 10:13 (GWT)

Wednesday

"Fear has the ability to make you foresee the imaginary as a reality."

Overcome fear by your faith. The evidence of faith is that the reality of what you cannot see is possible and tangible but never led by a spirit of fear. What God wants you to possess by faith He does not let fear be the first emotion that triggers the expectation of what is coming. If that is what you are feeling, that is not of God. There is an excitement that brings a sense of fear in earnest expectation but not in dread. Get fear out of the way and open your spirit to receive what God wants to gift to you.

Mary, the mother of our Lord, received some disturbing news in fear. She heard the angel say to her, "Fear not." Those words mean the world to us, especially when our natural response to disturbing news is to fear. But there was something wonderful coming into her life and through her body, which would become a blessing to the entire world. Can you imagine how she must have felt, hearing that she would be the one chosen by God and overshadowed by the Spirit to birth the Lord of life into a dying world? Extraordinary news at best! Thankfully, in Mary's situation fear did not drive her to foresee a condemnable outcome for her life because the angel's words of reassurance veiled any outcome that was contrary to the will of God for her life.

Exercise your faith in the face of fear and in the face of what makes absolutely no sense and watch what God will do! #itisinyourfaith #faithoverfear

"Teach me your way, O LORD, so that I may live in your truth. Focus my heart on fearing you."
—Psalm 86:11 (GWT)

Thursday

"That knock at the door of your heart? It's God.
Let Him in."
#knockknock

"Knock, knock."
"Who's there?"
"God."

"Hey God, why are you knocking? Don't you just walk through walls? Doors are not a hindrance for you. So why knock?"

Imagine this conversation with someone who does not understand the respectability of God. Yes, we know that if we believe, God does not need to knock on anything to gain access or entry into our lives. He does not need permission. But God also does not just invite Himself into our spaces. God wants to be invited into our hearts. Someone is asking why does God need an invitation? Well, let's think for a moment. God is above all people and all things. God has the power to do anything, but God chooses to reserve that power in ways we will never understand. The greatest power that God has reserved is the violation of the free will that God has given to us. Free will says that I have the ability to make a choice. If God takes away my choice, then I am under the complete control of God. God is not wanting to control our lives, instead guide them.

In thinking about choice, what if God wants to see what I will do with my power to choose? Does that make God less God in doing so? Now, think about the invitation to come into your life. God gave you life. Yes. God gave you the choice of how to live. Yes. But God wants you to invite Him to be a part of your life. Okay. Let me put it another way: Jesus died for the sins of the entire world. Jesus does not force us to receive what He has done against our will. We are presented with the opportunity to receive this salvation by the acts of accepting and confessing.

So, God is still waiting for that invitation. Now the next time God knocks, do not ask why God is knocking. Grant God entry.

"Listen! I am standing and knocking at your door. If you hear my voice and open the door, I will come in and we will eat together."
—Revelation 3:20 (CEV)

Friday

"The Word of God is necessary food.
Make sure you eat of it daily."
#nomalnourishment

T he scriptures talk about milk and meat. Milk is reserved for babes in Christ while meat is the food for the mature in Christ. We acquire both nourishment and strength to grant us power for daily living when we eat the word of God.

As a preacher, I ought not pick up the word when it is time to preach. I am doing a great disservice to the Spirit of God when I do so. I cannot expect to give to God's people the full experience of revelation power if I only read and study it when it is time to proclaim.

Malnourishment can lead to death; therefore, I need to daily intake the word of God so that I am not deficient in any way that will lead to the death of my spiritual life with God. We understand the correlation made between the natural and the spiritual. We are made up of both. In my natural body if I do not eat the right foods, and better yet, if I do not eat at all, I am in danger of becoming physically malnourished, which can lead to physical death. So, it is the same with the Spirit: eat right, live right. Where is your nourishment? It is in the word of God.

"If thou put the brethren in remembrance of these things, thou shalt be a good minister of Jesus Christ, nourished up in the words of faith and of good doctrine, whereunto thou has attained."

—1 Timothy 4:6 (KJV)

Saturday

"Another way to look at faith:
A presumptuous presupposing boldness on a Higher Power
that invisibly accesses the intangible and makes it possible."

H ebrews 11:1 says, "Now faith is the substance of things hoped for, the evidence of things not seen." Faith forces each of us to look way beyond what is tangibly within grasp. Faith pushes us to operate on a level of presumption because everything that has been created requires us to have a level of faith in what the created thing was created to do. For instance, when I go to the ATM to use my bank card, I am hoping that money will be drawn out upon my properly accessing my money through the machine. I really do not know whether the money will be dispersed. I hope that once I have done what I am able to that I will be able to make a withdrawal.

Everything in the natural realm has no relation to faith, unless we do presuppose that the manifestation of what we taste and handle can be acquired without the presence of the Higher One who is the motivating force behind faith. He speaks, it becomes. Thus, faith is born. It all stems from the Creator who is the reason why we have the concept of faith in the first place. Scripture clearly admonishes us to embrace faith since it gives us reason to hope and have expectation, even though none of us have seen God at any time. Nonetheless, we know He is real. The reality is this: God's intangibility so it appears, gives my faith the tangibility to be cognizant of God's presence, and thus I can receive the outcome I am expecting because of my faith!

"Faith is the reality of what we hope for, the proof of what we don't see."

—Hebrews 11:1 (CEB)

Sunday

"What happens on the other side of your obedience is up to God."

In the Baptist Church tradition, we sing the lyrics to a song: "trust and obey, for there's no other way, to be happy in Jesus, but to trust and obey." The songwriter's message is simple yet poignant: happiness can be achieved when we trust and obey Jesus.

Our problem is hearing the directive "to trust and obey," especially when we think about what it means to be obedient. We want to be in control of the outcomes. God admonishes us one way, but since we are too eager to find out the results, we miss our opportunity to be obedient.

We must learn that to experience all that God is, we must obey. If there were no afflictions, there would be no healings. If there was no sin, there would be no salvation. Is it not at the expense of sin that salvation came? Salvation comes because there was a need to be met. So, it is with obedience.

Let us follow through with obedience so God can demonstrate His power through us, rather than doing things our way and incurring God's wrath.

"Then Samuel replied, 'Does the Lord want entirely burned offering and sacrifices as much as obedience to the LORD? Listen to this: obeying is better than sacrificing, paying attention is better than fat from rams…'"

—1 Samuel 15:22 (CEB)

Monday

"I would rather be in trouble with man than in contention with God."

Remember the times when you did something wrong and you got into trouble with your parents? You dreaded the consequences of your actions. You did your best to avoid that encounter and bringing up what you did. Of course, with wrongs come consequences, including some form of punishment to correct actions.

Now let us look at this example in a similar light with God. Who wants to get a spanking from God? None of us has the ability to withstand the correction of God. To be in contention with God because we want our way is not only absolutely absurd, but also the most foolish decision any of us can make.

Being in trouble with God is something that none of us should desire. We should always aim to do our best to avoid God's judgment upon us. As Scripture states in Hebrews 10:31, "It is a terrible thing to fall into hands of the living God." It translates to "Who has the power to stand toe-to-toe or contend with God?"

If we have contention with man, we have God to help us. But when your issue is with God, who can you go to? So, think twice about how you deal with the Lord.

"Only by pride cometh contention: but with the well advised is wisdom."

—Proverbs 13:10 (KJV)

Tuesday

"Just one click can change your life."

When the devil presents temptation in an easily accessible way, don't take the bait. It may be a phrase in your email subject line, or a picture that pops up on your desktop. Avoid the "virus" that it represents because whatever is on the other side of the click is intended to infect you with an incurable disease—a vice that keeps infiltrating your mind, your spirit, and your heart. If you permit it, most likely you'll turn to self-medication in the hope that what you apply will work.

You are going to need something stronger than what you have been using. You need the Great Physician to step in and, with His healing balm, deliver you from this affliction that has infected your worship, your family life, your relationship with God, and your thought patterns—all of which you didn't anticipate but that is how Satan works; his approach is subtle and unassuming.

So, remember that one click can open up a whole other world you may not want to enter. #caution #getyourhandoffthebutton #oneclick

"For this cause, when I could no longer forbear, I sent to know your faith, lest by some means the tempter have tempted you, and our labour be in vain."
—1 Thessalonians 3:5 (KJV)

Wednesday

"It is more a risk that you take rather than a chance.
Risks can be strategic while chance is just that: chance!"

#risk

R isks are a part of our human condition. Love, faith, careers, investments, your very life are all risks. The truth of the matter is that we are surrounded by situations that require some element of risk. Some occur against our will and others because of our will. You ought to know which risks to take and the ones to avoid. Ask God to give you the wisdom to understand what is being risked during those moments that happen without our willingness or provocation and ask His protection to guard you against the negative effects of the risk.

Chance on the other hand is based on some kind of luck. I can take a chance on an opportunity of some sort that may not require much of an investment of my efforts. I can view chance as a happenstance that may not look like much is lost, should it not work in my favor.

Risks are not always bad. Just know which ones are being used to stretch or distress you. Chance I would avoid; it has the potential to draw you into habits that can prove detrimental to your willingness to trust in God.

"Throw your bread on the surface of the water, because you will find it again after many days."
—Ecclesiastes 11:1 (GW)

Thursday

The L Factor:
"Loving someone does not mean you have to lose yourself in them."

When you love someone, you are willing to become what they need without compromising who you are. We don't love in spite of who we are, but because of who we are. Didn't God do that for us? He becomes what we need and never loses sight of His identity and His authority. The Father gave us His Son to become God incarnate and God the Savior for the purpose of making us one with the Father again. Since we are created in His image and likeness, can we not demonstrate that in the same way? God never told you to lose yourself in any relationship. Although all relationships need adjustments, some of us lose our identities for the sake of holding onto the ones that make us believe we're in love. It is not until we have that "aha" moment and fully recognize that we are no longer the people we once were and begin changing back into our original identities that we understand our relationship with the people we were drawn to was not based on love but control. This should never happen when God identifies you and qualifies you in a relationship.

If we trust God to show us how to become the people we need to be, then we can successfully enter into mutual relationships based on respect and real love.

"A person who gains sense loves himself. One who guards understanding finds something good."

—Proverbs 19:8 (GW)

Friday

"Misery has taken up too much of your time."
#givemiserynospace

M isery was never meant to keep you company. It not only steals the company that you'd rather keep, but also replaces it with its wretchedness. I cannot stand being around miserable people. They suck all of the energy and life out of me. They force their misery upon my intimate space and expect me to join the bandwagon and become miserable as well.

If you stop and think about it, why would you be miserable when things are going well for you? Have you ever thought to yourself, "I am doing fine," then "Alice" comes around and all of a sudden, I feel horrible. I am grumpy, I have no patience, I snap at every little thing. Why? Misery has found a partner and, tag, you are it! So, what do you do?

When you see misery trying to steal your peace and joy and zap your strength, then you have to be deliberate in ensuring that misery can never attach its emotion to any part of your life. You have the power to make misery leave by choosing to think about something good. Why don't you try that some time? Too much time is spent accommodating misery when you should be making room for contentment.

"I will rejoice and be glad because of your mercy. You have seen my misery. You have known the troubles in my soul."
—Psalm 31:7 (GW)

Saturday

"God is in control; so, let Him take control."
#hearwhattheSpiritissaying
"Be still and know that I am God: I will be exalted among the heathen,
I will be exalted in the earth."
—Psalm 46:10

O ur human condition compels us to want to control everything. There may be a small population of individuals who do not want to control anything. This may be because they have not recognized the power that comes with control and being the decision maker in a situation, especially when the outcome is favorable. God teaches through our relationship with Him that He needs to be in control of our lives so that we are not recklessly making decisions and acting on those decisions while running the risk of destroying our lives and the lives of others. We must face the music that God is leading our lives. He deserves to have total dominion over us because He sees what our human eyes cannot see and knows what our human finite minds cannot comprehend.

Whatever matter that is pressing upon your heart right now, whatever situation that has jarred your memory to live in a past hurt, whatever the tempter is using to destroy you, you must remember that God is in control. You have made Jesus Lord of your life. This means that the Lord is responsible for taking care of you and your business. Take your hands off of what you feel only you can control. God would like to demonstrate His power in your situation, but it requires you to yield and trust the method He uses to bring you through it. I know it is challenging to think you are doing nothing when you relinquish control to God, but that is false. You are exercising faith and perpetuity in what seems to be taking a long time to change. Just be still and know that God is in control.

"But if God's Spirit lives in you, you are under the control of your spiritual nature, not your corrupt nature."

—Romans 8:9 (GW)

Sunday

H.O.P.E. (He Offers Peace Eternal)
"Constant peace is an unvarying state that never functions apart from eternal hope."

You have heard the phrase, Hope springs eternal. What could this possibly mean? Does it mean that hope and eternity are interconnected? Does it mean that I cannot really have hope unless I have the eternal present? Well, how about we look at hope from a different perspective. What if we saw hope as a means to point us to peace or shalom, where nothing is missing and nothing is broken.

When I say, "He offers peace eternal," I am suggesting that the Lord offers us an opportunity to experience an expectation of wholeness in our lives. True peace and eternal hope represent fulfillment and completion.

God desires to bring us into an eternal hope and constant peace. You and I should be looking forward with earnest expectation for the opportunity to see God's completeness in us. Therefore, I am trusting that what God already did is actually done. Any wholeness in me is a result of understanding that the Eternal one had everything to do with my becoming, and He will always finish what He commences.

"Lead me in your truth—teach it to me—because you are the God who saves me. I put my hope in you all day long."
—Psalm 25:5 (CEB)

Monday

Ministry Matters 101:
"Every disciple is not always a supporter;
some are supplanters who are sent to take you to your destiny."

E very ministry leader will have some Judases, Thomases, Peters, and Johns. Just know which ones belong in your interior and which ones to leave in the exterior. They are all needed in the maturation of your ministry. Jesus had an inner circle. Those who walked closely with Him and were there in His weakest and most triumphal moments were positioned there because of relationship and intimacy. Who have you become intimate with that is really supposed to be a part of your exterior? Then you wonder why the betrayal. You question their denial of you in certain ministry moments. Position yourself like John by becoming a trusted confidante of the Lord, and the Father will show you through His Spirit who to be connected to. Remember: John did not ruin the fellowship; he was given the responsibility to look after Jesus's mother. Jesus had an assignment to fulfill, and his first task was to show the disciples how to live through rejection, betrayal, and denial. Jesus successfully overcame all three right at the hands of supporters and a supplanter. It did not deter the ministry mission; it only brought to light the challenges that the disciples would face in growing the Lord's church in community.

Jesus knew who would be close and who would serve in proximity to purpose. Ask the Spirit for similar discernment so that when a situation arises within your ministry network, you are steadied and unbothered by the outcome. Your ministry assignment is greater than the expectation of supporters and supplanters.

> *"Rise up, let us be going; see my betrayer is at hand."*
> —Matthew 26:46 (ESV)

Tuesday

"For every departure in your life,
there is an opportunity for something beautiful to arrive."

We all have had that frustrating moment when we are waiting in line to enter an airport terminal. Sometimes if you are fortunate, you can qualify for PreCheck. When that occurs, you do not have to worry about taking off your shoes; you just walk through the metal detectors in order to gain access to the gates. And if you decide to travel with a carry-on, your carry-on must weigh a certain capacity in order to be considered a carry-on.

So, my question to you is this: what excess baggage are you trying to use as a carry-on that you clearly know will not allow you to fly? Empty your suitcase of your strongholds, false burdens, habits, vices, anything that keeps you from enjoying the flight. God wants you to land safely, and He desires that you embark on a new experience. Be committed to leave the excess baggage behind. Philippians 3:19 says, "forgetting those things which are behind, and pressing toward those things which are ahead, I press toward the mark for the prize of the high calling of God which is in Christ Jesus."

God gives good gifts to His children. God has something extraordinary awaiting your arrival to the new place. In fact, it is standing at the gate of your heart. Do you want to see what is on the other side of your struggles, then go with God. He is waiting on the runway of your life for you to fly with Him.

"O LORD, in the morning You will hear my voice; in the morning I will direct my prayer to You, and I will watch expectantly."
—Psalm 5:3 (MEV)

Wednesday

"Don't bring carnal weapons to a spiritual fight; you will lose."
#2Cor10:3-6

"We wrestle not against flesh and blood..." Paul tells us this in Ephesians 6:12. How, then, are we to fight? We must understand who we are fighting and what weapons we are to use. We are all engaged in a spiritual battle. When we deal with spiritual matters, there is no physical manifestation of what we are fighting. Sadly, too many of us do not recognize this, so we come fighting with carnal, fleshly weapons. Earthly weapons will do us no good in the spiritual realm. Jesus conquered earthly matters with a spiritual undertaking. And though He died in the physical, He resurrected in spirit! So, too, we need to recognize that our fight is not against human beings; our fight is against weapons that are sent by the enemy of our soul to take us out.

Paul talked about our warfare being waged against lofty arguments. Paul contended with words against the opponents of Christ. The main device he used to address these railing accusations was to cast down the thoughts that were working contrary to the power of God. We cannot stand against the devil and fight with our fists; we cannot fight with knives, guns, or any other earthly weapons. Another way to look at carnal weapons: those things connected to our emotions, weapons that drive us to respond emotionally. This will not work against the devil. We cannot fight him with our emotions. We must fight with our faith, our worship, our praise, our time with God, we fight with the word of God.

So, the next time you enter into a fight, beloved, make sure you show up to the event with the right equipment. God does not put you in battle for you to lose, but for you to succeed.

"Blessed be the Lord my strength, who prepares my hands to war and my fingers to fight."
—Psalm 144:1 (MEV)

Thursday

"The fight is never fair,
but it is fixed in your favor when God is your corner man."

My father is a former golden gloves champ. He once shared with me the rudiments of boxing. I learned how to bob and weave and to stick a jab. While eating dinner we watched a featherweight fight together. The fascinating aspect of the whole exchange was the way the two fighters worked the ring while their corner men shouted where to hit their opponents. Throughout the eight rounds of boxing, you heard the corner men shouting out instructions for their opponents to win the fight.

Well, we are in the fight of our lives, and the Holy Spirit—our Corner Man—wants us to win, but in order to win against our opponent, Satan, we have to hear what the Spirit is saying and follow through with the Spirit's directions. It is clear that Satan does not fight fair. He intends to destroy; that is how he operates. But we serve a God who will fix the fight so that we win, and the only way that can be achieved is if we hear the voice of the Spirit.

What has the Spirit been instructing you to do that you may have been ignoring? Get your head in the fight and pay attention to your opponent. You have the means to defeat him.

"You will not need to fight in this battle. Position yourselves, stand still and see the salvation of the LORD, who is with you..."
—2 Chronicles 20:17 (NKJV)

Friday

"God knows the amount of elasticity your life can handle.
Let Him stretch you!"

Who really wants to be stretched? Think about a brand-new rubber band. When you pull at it, it is difficult to expand. The more you use it, the looser it becomes and the stretching becomes easier. You and I are like that rubber band.

God has allowed some issues to come into your life to stretch you. Working with God, you come to understand that you will not snap because He is the one doing the stretching. You believe that as He stretches you, you cannot take it. Remember: He controls the elasticity because He made you and He knows what you are made of. You really can handle the stretching and when the stretching is done, you are going to be better. You are going to be stronger; you are going to be more apt to address everything that comes your way to break you.

Remember: you are the rubber band that can be wrapped around something you are holding together. Continue to trust God, and you will bounce back into shape after the Lord stretches you. You won't break, though you will be stretched by God. Be willing to be extended.

"But lift thou up thy rod, and stretch out thine hand over the sea, and divide it: and the children of Israel shall go on dry ground through the midst of sea."

—Exodus 14:16 (KJV)

Saturday

"You deserve to be happy (blessed), not satisfied but happy (blessed)."

You deserve to be blessed. God does not want you to be happy; He wants you to be blessed. Satisfaction does not necessarily make one happy. It makes one accept a state of momentary pleasure, which can leave just as quickly as it comes. Satisfaction cannot be an achievable mark when it comes to the believer. God wants to bring us into a place of being blessed. Blessed signifies the ability to reach a state of contentment that has nothing to do with circumstance.

Satisfaction is driven by circumstance. You can be satisfied with something because the circumstance produces that outcome. Being blessed would never let you be content with being conditioned by your happiness through a circumstance. Happiness or being blessed challenges you to not accept less than being blessed. Satisfaction says expect what is beneath God's best for you.

Do you want to be happy or be blessed?

"You will be blessed when you come in and blessed when you go out."
—Deuteronomy 28:6 (NIV)

Sunday

"The change you want to experience requires your willing participation from its inception to its fulfillment."

C hange is a part of life. If we want to grow, we must change. Oftentimes, we see ourselves in a different place, but do not want to make the investment to change. Change your trajectory; change your outlook; change your perspective. It requires your being willing to submit to the process that the Lord will use to change you. Your participation is required if you want to live a different life. Change cannot happen without you. You are the reason that change has an opportunity to alter your life into something better. From inception to fulfillment, you must allow change to do in you what only change can do—change you and propel you into what is forthcoming and can only be appreciated when you have allowed the change to take place.

"Do not conform to the pattern of this world, but be transformed by the renewing of your mind. Then you will be able to test and approve what God's will is—his good, pleasing and perfect will."
—Romans 12:2 (NIV)

Monday

"Just because you can't see Him, doesn't mean He ain't real."
#Godisreal

I remember as a child having lots of imaginary friends. I lived in a world of make believe because I spent most of my time by myself. In those imaginary friend moments within my thought processes, you would not have been able to explain to me that my imaginary friends were not real. Even though they lived in my mind, they were real enough for me to believe in their existence, especially since no one else could see them. Retrospectively, it sounds quite silly—this ability I had to live in this pretentious state, creating an imaginary world within my mind. The powerful aspect about this is how very real my imaginary world was in my mind. Even though you may not accept the fact that these imaginary friends existed, to me in my mind they did.

Now let us think about how people perceive God and His presence on the earth. How many people today believe that God is just an imaginary entity that we people of faith have created to validate the existence of someone greater than us to make sure that the world functions as it should? Let us be honest: no one has seen God at any time. Jesus was seen by men; but God and the Holy Spirit were seen by none. They were experienced by persons, but never seen. So, I pose the question to you: Does this now mean that God is not real because we cannot tangibly reach out and handle His personhood? Or does it mean that He is very real, but our ability to accept the reality of a higher being that has the world in the palm of His hand will not rest on imagination, but it is actualized in faith?

God is more real than our abiding human natures. It is the world that we cannot see that is more relevant and real than the one we are living in right now. If I am able to create a whole world in my imagination that seems just as real as the one I am living in right now, how much more can the God that we do not see be real enough to catapult this world into existence and give it shape, depth, and life? He is real whether you choose to believe it or not.

"In God, we live, move, and exist. As some of your own poets said, 'We are His offspring.'"
—Acts 17:28 (CEB)

Tuesday

"The future is really not as futuristic as we think.
God is eternal and ever present
and He mastered bringing the future into our now.
It is called prophecy."

When I hear the word "future," I think of forthcoming, not yet, on its way. In the mind of God, the future is in the present. But how can the future be now? When we go back to Genesis and God's creative power willing life to come into time, God brought the future into our present. When He saw the demise of man's nature, He placed an eternal promise in the womb of the woman with a prophetic word that "the Seed of a woman would crush the serpent's head" (Genesis 3:15). The seed God was referring to was Jesus. Jesus was not yet known as Jesus, but prophetically speaking, we see the forthcoming of Christ in the present reality of the woman. We did not know which woman it would be, but the fact that it is the seed is a foretelling of the Christ's redemptive work. The Lord confirms His word. We see the proof of it. The Book of Revelation tells us that "the testimony of Jesus Christ is the spirit of prophecy" (Revelation 19:10).

All of Jesus' story is an unfolding message of God's coming salvation. Aren't you excited to know that God's future is in your now? It is a prophecy; it is a promise of what is to come that is already in the mind of God.

"Whom having not seen, ye love; in whom, though now ye see him not, yet believing, ye rejoice with joy unspeakable and full of glory."
—1 Peter 1:8 (KJV)

Wednesday

"The eye of the beholder sees Beauty."

W hat is beauty? It is said to be in the eye of the beholder. God measures beauty out of what He sees in us, from the inside out. We measure what is on the outside without looking within. The Beholder says to us in Ecclesiastes 3:11a, "He made everything beautiful in its Time." You are beautiful because the Beholder says so; you are beautiful! Insight not eyesight. If you understand this, then what is your eye seeing? Your eye is seeing what the eye beholds externally, but the Beholder sees what is happening internally. True beauty is from within.

Our society pushes and brainwashes us to accept beauty as an externality that has no inner resolve to see beauty in its incomparable state. God does not want us spending our lives making ourselves up to be beautiful. Use that time to let the Lord bring out the beauty within you so that you may become what the Beholder sees before you even see it.

"Be beautiful in your heart by being gentle and quiet. This kind of beauty will last, and God considers it very special."
—1 Peter 3:4 (CEV)

Thursday

"If your soul is for sale, then sell out to Jesus."

W ho doesn't like a sale? Why purchase something full price when you can get it at a discount? What about your soul? The Bible says, "What does it profit a man to gain the whole world then lose his own soul?" (Mark 8:36). Ultimately, there is a profit to your soul being kept in the hands of Jesus, which begs the questions once again: And what about your soul? Should your soul be for sale? If it should be for sale, then who's buying it, and why have you priced it out?

Your soul is invaluable to the Lord. He said in the Scriptures that "we are to fear the One who can put the soul in hell; not fear man who can destroy the body" (Matthew 10:28). Your soul is to have a resting place. It is not an entity that has a price tag attached to it. It is a priceless piece of you that God alone owns. Therefore, look not to sell your soul to the devil or anyone else, but be sold out for Jesus! What Jesus promises is eternal rest for the soul. The devil, on the other hand, has an unending indebtedness that will never allow you to fully repay.

Remember: the devil does not want you to succeed. He wants you to suffer. What about your soul? Leave it in the care of the One who created you to have one.

My soul is not for sale to Satan! My soul is saved by the Savior.

"Our soul waits for the LORD; He is our help and our shield."
—Psalm 33:20 (ESV)

Friday

"Man's love leaves you mesmerized; God's love leaves you amazed."

Love is an emotion that can shipwreck you if you are not careful with its purpose for your life. When you meet someone and it is driven by love or at least you think it is, love can tantalize you and leave you in fantasy because man's love is operable in a vacuum of pretense. It is not until we have a meeting with God that the love we think blows our minds and rocks our worlds is displaced by the love that God gives overall.

The battle between eros and agape is in the degrees of demonstration. It is not until agape love overrides the perception that eros gives that we become amazed by what God's love feels like. Agape's influence on the spectrum of human love encapsulates the emotion of insatiability. Agape leaves you satisfied and content that God's love, which has no beginning and ending in steadfastness, is able to prove itself viable beyond human expression. God does not need us to create love but exhibit what has already been given and granted by the Superior One, who is love in so many ways beyond human comprehension.

"Who is a God like you, pardoning iniquity and passing over transgression for the remnant of his inheritance? He does not retain his anger forever, because he delights in steadfast love."

—Micah 7:18 (ESV)

Saturday

"You are called to build people not institutions!"

When ministry becomes more business than mission, we run the risk of treating God's people like transactions, rather than transformative people who have been empowered to build the kingdom of God. Beware of your motivation for building in the name of God and for God. God is the chief Architect. Only God knows what each building requires to stand on a firm foundation.

Jesus sending out the disciples on a mission did not require the disciples to physically build the Lord's church. They were called to build people. The ecclesia or the community of faith is established officially in the Book of Acts. But their time of communing with Jesus in the four gospels was a prelude to the business of building people. They had to learn the Lord's business plan of making disciples. Once they were empowered by the Holy Spirit, then they were released to go from place to place sharing the Gospel and creating communities of faith.

Let's make sure that we stay in line with the Lord's building practices. He is the One that will grant us to go ahead to fill the house.

"For we are God's fellow workers. You are God's field, God's building."
—1 Corinthians 3:9 (ESV)

Sunday

"What may be free for you, believe me,
someone had to pay for you to experience."

Everyone likes receiving something for free. If we are honest, everything that could be free for us to have, we would want. But has anyone stopped to think that because something is offered as free that there was no price to pay for us to receive it free? If a store is trying to increase sales and they offer to its customers "buy one, get one free" most often, people will take advantage of the deal because they are getting two for the price of one. This is costing the store owner some money either because they want to increase customer participation in the store to outshine their competitors, or they have to get rid of the items on the shelf in the store to make way for new inventory. Either way, we may get something for free either through a "buy one, get one free" purchase, or we may receive something for free at an event where vendors are trying to promote products. There could be any number of scenarios created to understand the concept of something being free. But remember someone had to pay for us to experience the ability to have something free.

Think about Jesus and what our Lord did for us. Our salvation is free but Jesus had to pay a price for us to experience this salvation. What did Jesus have to pay for? The wages of our sin. Jesus experienced mocking, beatings, shame, belittlement, ostracization, and a bloody crucifixion—all that we could have something for free. The Father made Jesus pay for our sins, not in a bad way, but in allowing Him to be the ransom on behalf of the world. Jesus willfully stepped in on our behalf. What He experienced we can never repay but have the opportunity to receive freely the gift of a new beginning—a new life now and one to come.

> *"For even the Son of Man came not to be served but to serve, and to give His life as a ransom for many."*
> —Mark 10:45 (ESV)

Monday

"Sometimes it is best to say nothing."
#silence

God made our mouths to close for a reason. At some point, the mouth has to shut for us to breathe through our nasal passages; to keep unnecessary matter from entering into our mouths; or perhaps just to be silent. How difficult it is for us to say nothing, especially in moments when you believe you have to justify your actions, explain yourself, prove someone wrong who thinks they are right, catch someone in a lie, point out someone's flaws and failures, stir up an argument because you like to argue.

What does the Bible say about being quiet? What did Jesus demonstrate in His earthly ministry before His accusers? There was a point when Jesus stood before the Sanhedrin and they asked Him questions and He did not say anything. When Jesus was defending the woman accused of adultery, caught in the act by her accusers, He stooped down and wrote in the ground and did not hastily say anything. Sometimes one must learn that silence is everything. Why? Because miscommunication only feeds into what was meant to be said but was not said, and sometimes the more one speaks, the worse it becomes.

Try being silent so that the atmosphere of words exchanged can be quieted. Try being silent so that you can hear what is being said and what is not being said. Try being silent because the Lord may want you to stop trying to have the last word. Your silence can very well become the last word. Be quiet, please.

"...a time to tear, and a time to sew; a time to keep silence, and a time to speak."

—Ecclesiastes 3:7 (ESV)

Tuesday

"You still have time to grow.
Just make sure you are going up in your growing."

A growth spurt can be a sudden surge in growth. It is said that kids have growth spurts. When you think about a growth, there is a certain level of increase or expansion. In regards to growing up or maturing, I would like to think of it as going upward. When we are infants, we are tiny in stature, and depending on your gene pool you may grow extremely tall or grow enough just to be considered the size of a family member. But the fact of the matter is that you are growing up. You are maturing.

In God, each of us has time to grow and to grow up. Life will present challenges that forces us to grow up. We may not want to experience growing up when difficulty occurs. We may want to experience growing up without the struggle. Sadly, we grow up when it gets rough. I just want to point you in the right direction as you are growing up. I want you to go up. The Lord sits above us and our going up and growing up is leading us up to where we belong.

So, do not allow anything or anyone to stunt your growth. People will tell the difference when we have grown up because there will be an upward mobility that cannot be denied by the person growing. You may feel taller on the inside. The situation that presented itself as something to stunt your growth, actually propelled it.

Bottom line, I hope you are going up as you grow up. I never knew of anything that grows downward.

"But solid food is for the mature, for those whose faculties have been trained by practice to distinguish good from evil."
—Hebrews 5:14 (NRSV)

Wednesday

"Are you purpose-driven or people-inspired?"

We are born with a purpose and for an intended outcome. This is how God created all of us. Somewhere along life's journey, we can easily become entangled in people and what people think, developing a false sense of inspiration, which lends itself to being people-inspired instead of purpose-driven. When we are driven, there is a passion that relentlessly wells up inside and we stop at nothing to see purpose fulfilled. But if I am people-inspired, that drive may not necessarily be motivated from a good place, and I run the risk of people controlling what my purpose looks like, or them hindering my purpose from coming forth because I sought inspiration and not purpose. If we are to desire inspiration as a means to push us, then that inspiration should come from the Holy Spirit whose motives are pure and noncontrolling, and then I can be motivated into purpose. Otherwise, anything other than the Holy Spirit's inspiration can take me out of the will of the Lord.

Ask yourself: What has been driving you and who has been inspiring you? If your answer is contrary to the Holy Spirit, then you are being driven by another force that will refute the power that is to generate your purpose and fuel your inspiration.

"Many plans are in a person's mind, but the LORD's purpose will succeed."

—Proverbs 19:21 (CEB)

Thursday

"The Kingdom will point you back to what's important."

When Jesus spoke of the Kingdom, He was trying to help us understand that we are living in the King's domain. If we are living in the King's domain, then we do not have time for trivial pursuits of flight and fanciful living as the world does. The kingdom reminds us that everything we will ever need to thrive on is found in the Hands of God and the Mind of God. We do not need to worry according to Matthew 6 about what happens in the kingdom. The kingdom shows us that we will not have to worry when our hearts are fixed on what God said and has already done. To say that the kingdom points you back to what is important is really God saying to us you have no time to waste pursuing earthly accolades that will not last well into eternity.

Jesus was so passionate about the Kingdom that He reminded us that if we are going to serve the Father, we must approach the presence of the Father with a kingdom mentality and a kingdom perspective. When it is all said and done, the kingdom in the life of the believer is a matter of the heart. There is no physical manifestation of the kingdom on earth. Just as I am admonished by the scriptures to hide the word in my heart, I am to think similarly of the kingdom!

"Seek the Kingdom of God above all else, and live righteously, and he will give you everything you need."

—Matthew 6:33 (NLT)

Friday

"Know when it is time to separate. Take a page from Abraham.
He and Lot could not walk together anymore.
Who are your Lots?"

S eparation may not be easy, depending on the context, but it is
necessary. Some of us enter into relationships, partnerships,
and alliances that God never ordained. We do not understand that
perhaps the reason it had not been working out is because there
was never to be an established connection. As we look at Abraham's
unfolding purpose, God called him to leave his father's house and go
to a place that God would show him. Never did God say to Abraham,
take family with you. Abraham was only supposed to be going with
his wife and that was it. Lot joined himself to Abraham, and as a
result, God brought a separation.

What would have happened if Abraham said to Lot from the
beginning, "You are not going"? He did not say it. Lot went, and then
as their clans became too large they had to separate. They could not
walk together anymore. Something changed; their goals looked very
different. God was speaking to Abraham and directing his steps. Lot
saw what looked attractive and pursued it. What would have happened to Abraham if he had followed Lot?

Learn a valuable lesson from Abraham's obedience to God. Know when it is time to part from persons that are not in alignment with your destination. Ask God to show you the Lots in your life. When He does, allow Him to do what you failed to: bring the separation.

"The Lord said to Abram after Lot had parted from him, 'Look around from where you are, to the north and south, to the east and west. All that the land that you see I will give to you and your offspring forever.'"
—Genesis 13:14, 15 (NIV)

Saturday

"Words have power."
"And you think your mouth is not a weapon for good or evil?
Think again and by the way think b4 u speak."

Words created the world in which we live. Look at the power of what God spoke into nothing. If God's words have that much clout, how powerful are the words you and I speak? They are so powerful that they can change minds, hearts, situations, directions. They have sheer power that can only be God-given. This is why Proverbs 18:21 tells us that "death and life are in the power of the tongue." What you and I speak can bring life or death. This means that our words are weapons of creative energy or diabolical demise. Good and evil come from our words.

So, the next time you want to say something, make sure that you think before you speak because we cannot take back what we say. What we speak can produce and what we speak can destroy. There is a reason why God allows our thoughts to be housed in our minds, before the mouth opens up to say something. We should think before releasing something that should be spoken out loud or kept in the safety of the mind. I am so glad God gives us options in moments like these. Choose the right one!

"Gracious words are a honeycomb, sweet to the soul and healing to the bones."

—Proverbs 16:24 (NIV)

Sunday

"Some of us need to stop lying by saying that 'the devil made me do it.'"

#really? #youdidit #Godgaveyoupower2overcome

The devil is the father of lies. This is what the Bible tells us. Therefore, I must ask a very important question: Why would the father of lies need your help? If he is the father of lies, he already knows how to do it well! So, why are you lying when you say, "The devil made me do it"? I want you to think clearly about this statement, because it says that a person is avoiding responsibility for their actions.

When you are a child of God, you are given divine help: the gift of the Holy Spirit, who reveals the truth so that you do not agree with the father of lies. It begins by being honest about your actions and recognizing that you do have some level of control and do not have to fall into the lie of the father of lies. You have an opportunity to be honest with God and yourself by saying, "It was me." Do you know how freeing that is?

You have power to overcome; God gave it to you. Use it and stop relying on the father of lies. He is already good at what he does without your help.

"...keep your tongue from evil and your lips from telling lies."
—Psalm 34:13 (NIV)

Monday

"Are you sitting on a landfill or a goldmine?
The exercising of your gifts will let you know what you have."

D umps are smelly and gory-looking places. They are filled with trash that is supposed to be processed to help our environment. But all it truly represents are waste areas. In New York there has been a fight for several years about the landfills that surround our neighborhoods. Our air quality is affected along with our water supply. In fact, a landfill is across town right off the highway in my community. So, as you can see, there is nothing good about landfills.

A goldmine, on the other hand, now that is something that we do not mind seeing in our midst. It represents opportunity, access, resources, wealth. People will dig for it; they will stop at nothing to reach it, even if it means taking it from someone else who has been sitting on it and doesn't have the necessary tools to acquire it.

Think about your gifts and ask yourselves this question: Which are you sitting on, a wasted gift or a gift that presents opportunity? God did not grant us gifts to be set upon a landfill. We are never to waste our gifts. They have been given for use, and good use at that. If you have not exercised your gifts for whatever reason, then you are allowing them to disintegrate into nothing instead of multiplying into more for the betterment of the kingdom mandate. Some of you are not even aware of what you have, hence the hesitation to step into your gifts.

Do you know that you are sitting on a gold mine? Do you know that your gift has the potential to be a great blessing to you and others? No more wasteful witnessing. It is your time to demonstrate the kingdom. The gold mine that you sit on is worth so much more than you realize.

"Even so you, since you are zealous for spiritual gifts, let it be for the edification of the church that you seek to excel."
—1 Corinthians 14:12 (NKJV)

Tuesday

"You have the power to write your story.
Just make God the Editor, Publisher, and Publicist."

So, I have been told that God should also write the foreword to your story. The foreword represents what we look forward to reading in a story. Who better to be the pen holder of your story but God, the One who knows you better than anyone else? People are quick to tell your story, and when they are given the power to do so, they can misrepresent it.

When God writes it out, He is editing, publicizing, and printing your story. He wants people to know your story. Allow Him to be your Ghost Writer, the Holy Ghost writer who pens what is necessary to be said.

A pen can be the most influential instrument to a piece of paper. Your life has been read by many already. Now, be sure to let what is read be written by you, and the changes completed by the Master Editor.

"My heart is overflowing with a good theme; I recite my composition
concerning the King; My tongue is the pen of a ready writer."
—Psalm 45:1 (NKJV)

Wednesday

Unconditional love above all:
"Though God has preconditions on His promises,
God's love requires no conditions!"

If the highest form of love is supposed to be unconditional, then why do we love with conditions when the love extended to us, undeserving as it is, loves us in spite of who we are.

Love says, "I love you, not because of what you do or don't do but because it is in my nature to love you. This is who I Am...Love. I embrace you with what others refuse to give you or choose to give you sparingly...Love. I created you to love. I created love to live in you so that you will recognize in the most unlovable moments of your life that Love comes to heal you, Love comes to affirm you, Love comes to embrace you, Love desires to reveal its all surpassing presence that teaches you how to love instead of hate. It is possible to love. Let no one tell you it is humanly impossible. I love because Love knows no other expression but to Love.

"Love will not deny itself the opportunity to demonstrate love, and its power is so mysteriously phenomenal that it will overtake a human heart without notice. Love invades when you want it to excuse itself. Love is bold and can never be watered down. Love has the ability to make you sane or insane if mishandled. But love is never to be held in only; it is to be given out. This is the only way we can see love break the conditional barriers of its recipients. I Am Love... and there is nothing you can ever do to prevent me from inviting you to be vulnerable in My hands. I make you weak but yet I give you strength. Don't deny me the right to love you the way I always envisioned. Just let me be...Love."

"We know how much God loves us, we have put our trust in his love. God is love, and all who live in love live in God, and God lives in them."
—1 John 4:16 (NLT)

Thursday

"Broken things can be mended, but sometimes the mending is invisible
while the scar leaves the memory of the brokenness."

#broken

W hen I think about something broken, it sometimes appears to
be irreparable. One thing we definitely know up front about
being broken is that something occurs that leaves a scar, a mar that
exposes the wound of what was made broken. A broken pot can be
put back together but you see the cracks, although held together by
some type of glue. The cracks are visible if you look closely. Further
proof that something is broken: when you try to fill the broken vessel
with something that is fluid enough to seep through the cracks.

Now, let us rethink about being broken, being irreparable with
the person who mends the brokenness. Let us presuppose that being
broken is not a bad thing. As a matter of fact, being broken can represent one who is usable in the Hands of God. Life scars cause brokenness, and as a result of those wounds, what was healed happens
internally while leaving an external picture of the wound that caused
the brokenness. It is a reminder that you survived the affliction, and
what you thought could not be made whole again is made whole
because someone saw your wounds not just as a scar, but proof of
your healing.

*"He heals the brokenhearted
And binds up their wounds."*
—Psalm 147:3 (NKJV)

Friday

"Fasting is not reflective of a facial expression.
It shows in the effort and in the outcome."
#doitinsecret

J esus tells us in Matthew 6:16 these words: "And whenever you fast, do not look dismal, like the hypocrites, for they disfigure their faces so as to show others that they are fasting." When we fast, we are not to adorn our faces, bring attention to others that we are fasting. We should not be walking around looking like death on limbs. We should not be looking like we just stepped out of one of those horror movies. Our faces should not be sunken in; lips dry; skin parched. We should not be looking as if we were on a 200-mile walk and we are about to shrivel up and die unless we get water. Basically, beloved, if we are fasting, the only ones who should know this are us and the Lord. If you have medical issues, then, yes, consult your doctor. Otherwise, it should not become a production that causes one to boast, as if fasting is some great feat that deserves a pat on the back.

When I fast, and when I pray, I go into a secret place with the Lord; I steal away with the Master and I pray and fast for direction, communion, instruction, power, understanding, wisdom. Whatever the outcome is, the release of the outcome is God's and God's alone. I make the effort by doing it in secret; I do it in a way that does not bring attention to myself or the mission. This way I gain my reward by being invisible with what is an intimate act of worship before the Father.

Jesus never announced that He was fasting. He doesn't spend time telling us about the times He fasted because that is not the important lesson we are to learn from His spiritual regiment. He tells us how not to fast, which means there is a proper way to do it. If Jesus showed us how by going away to a secret place to pray, then I am most certain He did the same with fasting. When He talked about fasting, prayer was mentioned. So, it is evident that whatever we do in fasting, must be done in secret, as He instructs us with prayer.

"Then I set my face toward the LORD God to make request by prayer and supplications, with fasting, sackcloth, and ashes."
—Daniel 9:3 (NKJV)

Saturday

"When you know who you are, then you are confident
while others are curious about who they think you are."

Jesus asked the disciples in Matthew 16, who were men calling Him to be? Jesus did not ask the question because He had an issue with who He was. He was asking to affirm before all of them who He was. In other words, Jesus already walked with confirmed heavenly authority, which is why He asked the question to make sure that the disciples recognized who was in their midst.

God can do the same with us. He gives us confidence that resembles Jesus and causes others to see it. Sadly, there are those who are too curious to recognize who we are in God; their curiosity prevents them from really seeing what God is revealing in their midst.

Never let anyone take away your confidence in Christ. He called you before time began and gave you a name and a purpose to fulfill. If you find yourself around people who are spending unnecessary time trying to figure out who you are, then their curiosity will rob them of a unique opportunity to know you in a way that God desires. Walk in confidence of what God already said about you. Jesus did, and when the religious leaders questioned His identity by saying, "Isn't that Joseph the carpenter's son?" Jesus did not allow their curiosity to deter His purpose. Over time, He demonstrated that He was so much more than a carpenter's son; He is the Son of God. The more men and women began to exclaim loudly and publicly who Jesus was, the angrier the curious ones became.

Never worry about what the curious ones may be thinking or saying about you. When you know who you are, you will handle them and their accusations and presumptions differently. Learn from Jesus's exchange with Peter in Matthew 16:16–17: "And Peter replied, 'Thou art the Christ, the Son of the living God.' Then Jesus said, 'Flesh and blood have not revealed this to you, but My Father which is in Heaven.'"

"I did not know Him; but that He should be revealed to Israel,
therefore I came baptizing with water."
—John 1:31 (NKJV)

Sunday

"Stop worrying about who left. Just close the door behind them."
#that'sall

N o one likes it when people you expect to stay walk out of your life. It hurts and it sucks. But if they left because they did not want to be there anymore; if they left because they have found something better; if they left because it was just time to go, then stop worrying about them.

Doors are meant to be opened and closed. Doors are closed to keep out unwanted things and persons. Your life was never meant to be an open-door policy for people to prance in and out. You want those who God sent into your life; everyone else can walk out the door. Just get up and close the door, physically and mentally. Leave no access for a return.

I love the movie, *The Devil Wears Prada*. Meryl Streep plays a character named Miranda. Miranda is sophisticated. Some would even say evil though straightforward. She would give instructions and then close by saying, "That's all." In other words, "Leave my presence." Some of you need to have a similar attitude. No need to cry over it or them any longer. Just say, "That's all."

"Get wisdom, get understanding: forget it not; neither decline from the words of my mouth."
—Proverbs 4:5 (KJV)

Monday

*"Some lessons you have to learn and carry forward
while others you can abandon
and leave them right there where you learned it."*

L essons are given to be learned. At some point, a lesson learned should become a lesson mastered. You really do not want to repeat a lesson. You want to learn it the first time and move on to the next one. Life is full of lessons. Sadly, we do not always learn them the first time around. Sometimes it takes more than one time. It may take several times, but the lesson will eventually be learned.

As you learn the lesson, ask God to identify those lessons that you need to carry with you along your purpose. Those others that you learned can afford to stay right where you learned it. You were just meant to learn it, not carry it on your journey, not lodge in it or log it in your mind. Learn it and move forward. Those lessons you are supposed to carry forward may very well be used to help someone else. Ultimately, the goal is to learn your lesson and learn it well that you may teach others how not to repeat their mistakes.

*"Teach me thy way, O LORD; I will walk in thy truth: unite my heart to
fear thy name."*
—Psalm 86:11 (KJV)

Tuesday

*"God's silence does not mean disinterest in your situation.
You and He can't talk at the same time. Someone has to listen."*

It would be wonderful in another world to be able to talk and listen at the same time. Sounds like it would be confusing, like gibberish almost. If you are in conversation with someone, it should mean that at some point you are speaking and then listening.

When talking with God, we tend to do most of the talking. First of all, God already knows what we are going to say to Him. How about we cease talking so that we can hear Him? We need to hear what He is saying because if He is not talking, then we will not know what important information or instruction He wants to release. He speaks so softly to us that if we are not careful, we will completely miss what He wants to convey.

We cannot talk at the same time God is talking. We need to be listening. Someone has to. It might as well be you since you need what God has to offer.

"Even the wise could become wiser by listening to these proverbs. They will gain understanding and learn to solve difficult problems."
—Proverbs 1:5 (ERV)

Wednesday

"Who's in your family?
Dream killers are relatives to envy and jealousy.
Have no part in those family members."

We have all types of folks in our families. There are those we absolutely adore, and then there are the ones we can afford to see once a year at the annual family gathering. When we think about family support, it should be a welcoming presence. There is nothing like having family stand with you and encourage you; however, if they are dream killers, steer clear.

Joseph was a wonderful example of how to deal with family members. His brothers despised his gift and they despised his relationship with their father, Jacob. So, when God gave Joseph two dreams and he shared them with his father, somehow the dream killers tried to enter the picture with their envy and jealousy. His brothers displayed envy and jealousy by trying to get rid of Joseph. Little did they know that the dreams Joseph had were greater than their envy and jealousy. Those dreams represented a deeper purpose that God had ordained for the nation of Israel, His people. So, the dream killers were unsuccessful in their quest to destroy the dream and the dreamer.

If you find yourself experiencing a similar account, have no dealings with those family members. Avoid their desire to destroy what God said. They will not succeed unless you allow them to defeat you. When God gives a dream, He will see to it that it comes to pass.

As you think about your family members that are relatives to envy and jealousy, just love them right where they are and maintain your integrity through it all. God is dreaming for you and showing you what you can become, if you believe the dream and defy the dream killers.

"Come now, let us kill him and throw him into one of the pits. Then we will say that a fierce animal has devoured him, and we will see what will become of his dreams."
—Genesis 37:20 (ESV)

Thursday

"The alabaster box had a cost.
Don't waste that oil on anything or anyone."
#guardyouroil #stewardship #whatareyoupouring?

Mary's sacrifice at the feet of Jesus is perhaps the most powerful transitional moment in the foretelling of Jesus's walk to Calvary. He had to be prepared. He had to be anointed. This is not to suggest that Jesus was not already anointed, but if you remember—to fall in line with scripture and its fulfillment—Jesus said that Mary's demonstration of love by pouring expensive oil on Him would go down in history. So, if Jesus can say that Mary's act of love poured out on Him can go down in history, why do we treat the anointing so frivolously as if there is no oil or sacrifice?

The anointing of oil and the smearing of the sweet scent of power and presence upon us does not belong to us. The oil is the Lord's. The oil is representative of the Spirit of God upon us to do the work of ministry.

If you understand this, then make sure you are not pouring your oil out on those who cannot relate to the symbolism of what the oil means. Do not allow anyone to waste God's oil for no reason. What you are pouring out will certainly determine what you shall become when the smoke clears and the dust settles. You are more valuable than you even realize and what is on you confirms it. #guardyouroil

"There were some who said to themselves indignantly, 'Why was the ointment wasted like that? For this ointment could have been sold for more than three hundred denarii and given to the poor.' And they scolded her. But Jesus said, 'Leave her alone. Why do you trouble her? She has done a beautiful thing to me.'"

—Mark 14:4–6 (ESV)

Friday

*"Don't let the weak areas of your life
override the untapped areas of who you are!"*

I wish we all had abilities that would never question our inade-
quacy of potential. Superman was powerful, but when he saw
kryptonite something happened that he lost control. Superman
became weak and ineffective. He was of no use to anyone. Similarly,
if we allow our weaknesses to overshadow our untapped areas and
our potential, a type of kryptonite can immobilize us.

Superman's cape and red boots were symbols of power. When he
flew in to save the day, people mentioned the S on his chest and most
likely the red cape and boots. He looked powerful, and his power was
always on display when the kryptonite was not near him.

We have kryptonite called self-condemnation that we wear so
well. We would love to escape it; we desire to rid ourselves of it. If
only we would not magnify our weaknesses by our poor choices, our
vices, and habits that we keep repeating, then the kryptonite would
not overpower us and zap us of our strength. The weaknesses we display encourages more people to pay attention rather than foreseeing
the untapped areas of our lives.

We all may have been guilty at one time or another. Let's reverse
the verdict on our untapped areas by giving enough evidence that

says we are not guilty of being weak. We have yet to prove to our untapped areas the endless possibilities of the "overcoming power" in our midst.

So, what is stopping you? What makes you weak that does not have the power to keep you weak unless you allow it? Reach for the word of God. Jesus does not condemn, so do not condemn yourself. He is our Savior, our Hero...no red cape and boots, but a crown, a robe, and a bloody cross that proves He took what appeared to be weak to give us strength. The untapped area is the strength waiting to burst forth in power, and that strength begins to manifest itself when we stop looking at what makes us weak and turn our attention to what gives us strength.

"Yes, I am glad to be weak or insulted or mistreated or to have troubles and sufferings, if it is for Christ. Because when I am weak, I am strong."
—2 Corinthians 12:10 (CEV)

Saturday

"Have no regrets over relationships that fall like leaves.
The winds will whisk them away, and soon spring will make room for new!"

I love the fall. It is a picture of beauty as you see the leaves change colors. Some people hate the idea of having to rake up leaves from the ground because the leaves belong on trees. But as the trees become barren because winter is coming, one starts to think differently about the scenery.

Some of our relationships end up in a similar vein. What was once beautiful to behold has now become cold and lifeless, it seems. Do not envision this moment when the leaves depart as something regrettable. It is an opportunity for something new to burgeon. Seasons give us hope to see transformation in action, and we have no control over when it appears. We are to accept that a season is ending and another beginning. When this occurs, keep your eyes on what once looked hopeless and empty, now appearing full of light and color. The leaves have fallen, but there is room for new ones to appear. Welcome the new.

"Behold, I will do a new thing; now it shall spring forth; shall ye not
know it?"
—Isaiah 43:19a (KJV)

Sunday

"Every response does not have to require words."
#learnthelesson

H ave you ever been in a conversation with yourself because the other person decides that you are not worth the response? You become frustrated because you desperately want the conversation to continue, but they have decided to check out. Instead of being angry with them for being silent, learn the lesson that every response does not require your words.

Silence is a powerful mechanism for acquiring peace amidst confrontation or difficult discussions. Silence is a deafening revenge to words spewed in anguish. Become content with reserving your words, because when you reserve your words, you reserve your reaction, which can become more harmful to you than the one who went silent on you.

"People used to listen to me, the sense of expectation visible on their faces; they waited in silence for my advice."
—Job 29:21 (The Voice)

Monday

"You want God to hold your hand when He is trying to release you to fly!"

God is an incredible pilot and navigator. He has already prepared you to be successful in this next endeavor, but you are still trying to hold His hand as you stand on the mountain's edge of destiny. There is that moment when having a hand to hold reinforces security and safety, but the hand holding can also intervene with the takeoff. God knows how much of His presence and support you will need. When it is time to fly, expect less hand holding and more vocalizing of your instructions to move! Do not resist the urge to hold onto His hand. He will not allow it because He knows you are more ready than you realize.

Here's another way to look at it: I used to make paper airplanes in class; depending on how accurate my lines and folds were, the more successful the takeoff. When I released it from my hands into the air, it soared for a short while until it landed. You are that paper airplane that God has constructed to fly. You have to be released from God's hand in order to see how far you can go. Soar!

"But those who trust in the Eternal One will regain their strength.
They will soar on wings as eagles."
—Isaiah 40:31a (The Voice)

Tuesday

"Loving past one's pain is healing."

Love and pain are not synonymous. They just happen to end up in the same landscape of human emotion. Pain and healing would seem to work in congruence with a better outcome in one's situation. So, loving in a painful moment requires a lot of healing, and this healing cannot be measured. The power of your healing is your ability to not allow pain to imprison you, hence the job of love. Love forces you to experience healing from what often appears insurmountable, especially if you see the pain as being too great or severe. The power of healing and the power of love will anesthetize the pain. You have a right to healing, and love will lead the way if you allow it.

Jesus is the absolute example of love and healing. The pain He endured for us yet the healing that stems from that pain is Love! John 3:16 says, "For God so loved the world that He gave His only Begotten Son that whosoever believeth in Him shall have everlasting life."

The love that God gave to the world was the sacrifice of Jesus Christ. The brutality and maligning that He endured at the hands of His oppressors was painful, but love made it worth every scourge. If God can accept the verdict of His Son's death by crucifixion and allow this to be the act of love, then our healing is possible. Remember: Jesus rose after all He endured. And in that you will find your Healing.

"But for you who fear my name, the Sun of Righteousness will rise with healing in his wings."
—Malachi 4:2a (NLT)

Wednesday

"Your experiences do not make you an expert.
If you can accept the lessons,
then they'll teach you to learn from the encounter."

E xperienced or experts. What are we? Some of us believe that we are the wise ones to speak to a matter because of an experience. The experience was just that: an experience. I was taught that the experts are persons who have studied a craft and have mastered outcomes in that craft, understanding that other outcomes can arise. One encounter with a situation will not make you a master. Mastery takes time, and an experience already shows the limitation of time.

Use the experience to learn from the experience and be prepared to receive the lesson that goes along with the encounter. If you deem yourself an expert out of an experience, then you have not really learned from the encounter; you spend more time focusing on being the expert, and the experience becomes something you believe you have conquered.

"Let my teaching fall on you like rain; let my speech settle like dew.
Let my words fall like rain on tender grass, like gentle showers on
young plants."
—Deuteronomy 32:2 (NLT)

Thursday

"Beware of those who have more answers to your problems
than their own."
#tellthemthanksbutnothanks

I am leery of persons who always want to give you advice. You have watched them in matters of their own affairs only to see that what they have applied to their own lives is not working out. So, why are they so eager to give you advice when it is apparently unproven? Oftentimes we are not sure what the answer should be. But anyone who is adamant that they know exactly what you need to do, what actions you ought to take can begin to play the role of God in your lives. You do not need another God. The Father is very clear in how He directs your steps.

Prepare the person who refuses to take an introspective look at themselves by gently inviting their non-participation in the affairs of your life. God knows what advisement to give to you on any given matter. You may have attempted to appreciate their input but it is interfering with God's response. If they become angered by your unwillingness to receive their advice, remind them that their advice has human limitations, and you choose to trust in the limitless wisdom of God.

"If you need wisdom, ask our generous God and he will give it to you.
He will not rebuke you for asking."
—James 1:5 (NLT)

Friday

"God's way of forgetting is a permanent cancellation
from the memory of His Omniscience."
#somebodysaycancel #erased #thankyouJesus

While I was at the copy machine today making duplicates for an appointment, the machine ran out of paper. As a result, I had to cancel everything in the memory of the machine that was prepared to spit out what I needed for my appointment. In that moment, though it was not a great revelation, I thought to myself, "Wow, just like that, what I intended to be duplicated is completely erased the moment I hit the cancel button."

The beauty of the cancel button was that the machine asked me a very important question before I selected ok: "Are you sure you want to cancel?" I hit ok, and just like that, no memory of the original document was found in the system's memory card. Well, God does the same thing for us. Imagine all the images the devil wants to duplicate in your mind over and over again; page after page spits out and it seems like the pages will never stop. But if God steps in and stops the reproduction of the condemnation the devil wants you to keep seeing, then we ought to celebrate this divine interruption that hits "cancel" on your records.

God does not need to keep seeing page after page of what we

have done. Jesus paid that price already, and I am so grateful tonight that there is a "cancel" in our presence that has taken the power of condemnation away from the devil. It is gone—what you and I have done. God erases and it is nowhere to be found.

So, start appreciating yourself, and stop allowing yourself to be beaten up over what you did. God already knows. We don't have to ask God the question, "Are you sure you want to cancel?" Jesus took care of that when He allowed His cleansing blood to be poured out of His body on Calvary.

Now that God has hit cancel on your sins, you need to hit the cancel button on those relationships that want to keep those parts of your life duplicating what God has already erased. Don't stack the paper in the feeder of your mind anymore. Don't press start. Remove the paper, and, if possible, shred it from your heart, your spirit, and your mind. Let there be nothing for the devil to put together again. It is all a waste.

"Fear not, for you will not be ashamed; be not confounded, for you will not be disgraced; for you will forget the shame of your youth, and the reproach of your widowhood you will remember no more."
—Isaiah 54:4 (ESV)

Saturday

"Pointing fingers of condemnation will never be greater than nail-pierced hands of salvation."

Living in an accusatory world is a very condemning practice for those who love to hurl accusations. But no matter how often you find yourself under the microscope of finger pointing, the work of Jesus on the cross far outweighs every hurled stone, in the form of words, at your life. No one likes to feel the piercing words of condemnation, but the beauty of what Jesus has rendered through His work on the cross is the most powerful weapon against words of destruction.

The nail-pierced hands of Yeshua have enough power to heal every wound words have made. Who knew it best but Him? You heard His words from the Cross. He said it to heaven while perhaps reflecting on every condemning word spoken in the midst of His miracles, signs, and wonders...He said it to heaven as those words turned into wounds that they beat into His beautiful, bloody body. He said, "Father, forgive them for they know not what they are doing" (Luke 23:34).

There will never be enough finger pointers to counter the nail-pierced hands of our Loving Savior. Even those finger pointers will one day lift hands willfully in reverence or clutch their fists in angst because they refused to receive the healing hands of the only One who can save their souls.

> *"And the free gift is not like the result of that one man's sin. For the judgment following one trespass brought condemnation, but the free gift following many trespasses brought justification."*
> —Romans 5:16 (ESV)

Create a prayer log!

"Prayer is your conduit to a variety of outcomes that are God led and God inspired. It is a necessity of the spiritual journey of knowing God and self."

Sunday

Monday

Tuesday

Wednesday

Thursday

Friday

Saturday

Sunday

Monday

Tuesday

Wednesday

Thursday

Friday

Saturday

Sunday

Monday

Tuesday

Wednesday

Thursday

Friday

Saturday

Sunday

Monday

Tuesday

Wednesday

Thursday

Friday

Saturday

Sunday

Monday

Tuesday

Wednesday

Thursday

Friday

Saturday

In Closing

L ord, I ask that You allow these words that I have penned to touch someone's life in a special way. Life is difficult at times and sometimes forces us to chew what it gives. Allow us to see that You never give us more than we can bear. I pray that You are someone's light in darkness, someone's hope in despair, someone's peace in chaos, someone's love in war. You bless us with your Light. You have called us to be salt in your world. Show us the picture of beauty that you have created in us, for Your word tells us that we are fearfully and wonderfully made in Your image, the Imago Dei.

I pray that those who have followed my words through the years and those who will now discover them, will see an opportunity to fulfill their dreams and visions by taking a moment to search for You. For when they search for You with their whole hearts, as the scripture says, they will find You.

You have given my words life. Now, send these words to the brokenhearted, send these words to those in fear, send these words to those who are uncertain about who they are and what You have called them for. Let today be the best day of each day for them. Thank You for living in me and sending these words out in your world to help someone see a brighter tomorrow.

In Jesus's Name, I pray. Amen.

God bless you my dear ones! Read, Write, Reflect!
Kimberly V. Headley, Author

About the Author

K imberly Headley is a minister, teacher, poet, playwright, and entrepreneur. Kimberly has done mission work in George, South Africa, and has ministered on the streets of New York City, sharing a message of hope and healing. She believes in the power of words and understands that one's thoughts shape the world in which one lives. Kimberly's life ambition is to empower others to realize the presence of the Imago Dei (the Image of God), recognizing that they have been created with a divine purpose.